The Winston Grammar Program

BASIC LEVEL
Teacher's Manual

Paul R. Erwin

Precious Memories Educational Resources
18403 NE 111th Ave
Battle Ground, WA 98604
(360) 687-0282

Printed in U.S.A.

ISBN 1-889673-02-1

The contents of *The Winston Grammar Program* are fully protected under the patent laws of the United States.

Contents

A Note to the Homeschooling Parent. . .

The following is a suggestion for using Winston Grammar with your child. In general, children develop abstract thinking skills around 9-11 years old so the most ideal time to teach grammar is fifth or sixth grade. Because grammar is composed of mostly abstract concepts, children who have not yet developed their abstract thinking skills will often have more difficulty with it; most parts of speech have no meaning to their world. Nouns are relatively easy because they play with toys and crayons, etc. Action verbs are not too difficult because they can relate to running and jumping. Articles are just plain easy. Adjectives also don't pose too hard a task as children can relate to something that's blue, green, big or little. So if you are teaching a third or fourth grader, expect these things to go relatively quickly. Beginning with adverbs, children often get bogged down. The natural tendency is to move ahead anyway, thinking that there will be lots of practice before the end of the book. However, if a child doesn't thoroughly understand adjectives and adverbs, then when s/he gets to prepositional phrases, s/he meets an impasse trying to figure out if the phrase is used as an adjective or adverb. This is also true when it comes to deciding about a word being an adjective or a predicate nominative if it follows a linking verb. The plan we suggest will help prevent some of these frustrations. Plan to do each worksheet over a number of days. Do 2-3 sentences each day so that the child has to review the concept several times before the worksheet is complete. This should only take 5-10 minutes to do. Then spend 2 or 3 days having your child find that part of speech in a paragraph or two of his/her reading. When that is easy, ask for that part of speech in his/her writing. No matter what s/he is writing, usually you could ask for 5 adjectives or 3 direct objects, etc. Have your child underline them so that you <u>know</u> s/he did it purposefully and it wasn't just an accident that the part of speech got there. This is the part where the child who hasn't developed abstract thinking gets stalled. S/he will stare out the window or give a million excuses why s/he can't do this. You may give some help with it for a day or two, but before you move on to the next worksheet, the child should be able to do this exercise. If a child cannot use the part of speech, then the concept has not been integrated into his/her understanding. Moving on will just cause bigger frustrations in future worksheets. If you are working with a younger child or with any child who needs more practice, consider getting the Basic Supplemental Workbook. It will give you an extra worksheet for each one in the Basic Program.

While this may not be the lesson plan for everyone, it is a plan for teaching grammar in a less stressful manner, generally taking more than a year to complete the Basic Level. Feel free to call us with any comments or questions you have along the way. We will be glad to talk to you.

Introduction

Purpose and Method of *The Winston Grammar Program*

The purpose of *The Winston Grammar Program* is to help students understand the structure of language and comprehend the principles of traditional grammar. The Basic Level teaches the parts of speech, prepositional phrases, modification, and noun functions. Its methods are designed to produce thorough, pleasant, effective instruction—the kind that creates feelings of success in school.

The Winston Program uses innovative means to achieve conventional ends. It does away with the traditional grammar textbook, lecture approach, and heavy emphasis on rote memorization. Instead, it gives students a set of color-coded clue cards and a book of exercises which together generate multi-sensory activities: moving, seeing, hearing, speaking. Repeated use of the cards results in the students' acquisition of knowledge with little or no memorization required.

Materials for the Basic Level

Teacher's Manual
Student's Workbook
Manipulatives (color-coded clue cards)

Contents of This Manual

The directions in this manual show teachers how to prepare students to analyze the sentences on each of the thirty worksheets contained in the Student's Workbook. In this program, a lesson should be considered as both the teacher's presentation of the information that students will need for a given worksheet and the students' analysis of sentences on the worksheet.

Procedures

In *The Winston Grammar Program*, learning is incremental. Parts of speech, prepositional phrases, modification, and noun functions are taught in a controlled sequence with built-in review. Central to the program is the fact that no word is a part of speech until it appears in the context of a sentence. Students may need to be reminded of this occasionally.

Each lesson should begin with a teacher's presentation of the information that students need for a given worksheet. The cards that students should have in hand to begin the lesson and the new concept to be taught are named at the top of each new set of directions in this manual. In most cases, the teacher should begin by explaining both sides of the card(s) shown on the page and the ideas contained in the section called "Important Information for Students." The clue side of each card provides clues for identifying within a sentence the part of speech named on the reverse side. The reverse side of the card names the part of speech, gives the symbol or abbreviation for it, and in some cases shows its function or its role as a modifier.

Directions include sentences for teachers to use as preparatory material before students proceed to a particular worksheet. Such sentences should be presented both orally and visually on a chalkboard or an overhead projector, and students and teacher together should analyze these sentences, first using clue cards and then symbols and abbreviations.

The format of the directions for Worksheet 1 is different from what is found in the rest of this manual. It models a lesson for teachers by presenting a fairly comprehensive sample script as well as specific directions for activities. As directions in the manual proceed, they become less detailed because many procedures should become routine and, therefore, not require repeated explanation.

When a teacher completes the preparatory activities for a particular lesson as they are described in this manual, the students should be ready for the worksheet for the same lesson. Each sheet contains sentences for students to analyze. They do this first by using color-coded clue cards to identify parts of speech in a worksheet sentence. Each time they name a part of speech, they place the appropriate card on their desk. Ultimately, they create a horizontal pattern of cards, with each card representing a particular part of speech in the worksheet sentence. Next, the students transfer their knowledge about the same sentence to the worksheet where it appears. To do this, they label the words in the sentence, using abbreviations and symbols contained on the cards.

The activities of *The Winston Grammar Program* lend themselves to whole class, small group, or individual instruction. (Some older students or adults could teach themselves by using this manual along with the workbook.) Teachers of groups will find that use of the cards encourages students to stay involved and work all together on the same thing. In such a situation, the teacher's role is often that of a catalyst, causing students to think and act in a particular direction. As students use the cards and respond to the prompts of the teacher and each other in order to analyze the sentences, the teacher can immediately see how everyone is doing simply by looking around at the card patterns on the students' desks.

Sometimes the teacher will become a reacting observer rather than a discussion leader. In such cases, the teacher should react by leading a student to find an answer on her own rather than give it to her. For example, if a student says that *quickly* is an adjective in the sentence *Stan went to the store quickly*, the teacher should not say, "No, *quickly* is an adverb." Instead, the teacher should ask, "Why is *quickly* an adjective?" and the student, looking at the clue card for adjectives, should see why *quickly* is not an adjective in the given sentence. If the student then looks at the adverb clue card and responds that *quickly* is an adverb, the teacher should ask the student to use the clues on the card to explain why *quickly* is indeed an adverb.

Teachers who work with groups may want to use the Mastery Approach to learning. This method allows students to move to a new level only when they demonstrate that they have mastered the material for their present level. Nouns must be mastered, for example, before pronouns are considered. Likewise, students need to work on a particular area only until they demonstrate that they have mastered it.

The pretest and posttest provide teachers with a means of assessing students' skills on the concepts taught in the program. The pretest is meant to be given to an older student who has been taught some grammar in the past as an assessment of their current knowledge. It is not used for beginning students. The four quizzes are to be taken at regular intervals throughout the program. A bonus question at the end of each quiz challenges the student by presenting an item that is more difficult than the others on the same quiz.

Use of Materials

Sentences in the Teacher's Manual and on the worksheets in the Student's Workbook are designed to offer confusion-free practice and sidestep frustration by avoiding grammatical irregularities and exceptions. Teachers who want to maintain this condition should stay with the surface structure of the program's sentences if they wish to create additional sentences for students.

Students should use the clue cards to analyze sentences at least until all the parts of speech have been introduced. Procedures for the worksheets may vary. Students may individually mark their worksheets with symbols and abbreviations, or they can respond orally, work in teams, and so on.

Sequence of Topics

Directions

WORKSHEET

CARDS: Article, Noun, Blank
NEW CONCEPTS: Articles, Nouns

Article Card
(Clue Side)

> a   an   the

Article Card
(Reverse Side)

> ✔
> article

Noun Card
(Clue Side)

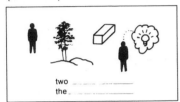

Noun Card
(Reverse Side)

> <u>noun</u>
> proper   common
> S., D.O., I.O., O.P., P.N., App., N.D.A.

Ask students to make three stacks of cards on the work surface in front of them. There should be a stack for the Article Cards, a stack for the Noun Cards, and a stack for the black Blank Cards. (These are the only cards that students will use in this lesson.) Clue sides for the cards in these stacks should be facing up.

Explain the cards using something like the following script.

Possible script:

Each kind of card that you have stands for a different part of speech.

Look at the clue side of an Article Card. It shows you the three words in our language that are articles: *a, an, the.*

The reverse side of the Article Card tells you that when one of these words appears in a sentence, it is an article. It also tells you that the symbol for an article is a check (√).

The Article Card is red to signal that a noun will closely follow it, although the noun may not be the very next word.

The clue side of the Noun Card shows you two things:

1. It shows four picture clues that tell you that nouns name *persons, places, things,* or *ideas*.

2. The bottom of the clue side of the Noun Card shows you two words.* The word *two* tells you that it makes sense to make a noun plural.

> *Example:* person   two persons

_____

* The clue words *two* and *the* at the bottom of the Noun Card will work with most, but not all, nouns.

A helpful hint about nouns is: you can count nouns.*

The bottom of the clue side of the Noun Card also indicates that it makes sense to say the word *the* in front of a noun in a sentence.*

The reverse side of the Noun Card tells you that the symbol for a noun is a single line beneath the word.

The additional information on the reverse side of the Noun Card will be discussed later.

The black Blank Card is used to mark any part of speech not yet introduced.

Model Lesson

Using an overhead projector or a chalkboard, present the following sentence:

    The boy and the girl saw a man eat an apple.

Possible script:

There are eleven words in the sentence. On your desk, you will put down an Article Card (clue side up) for each article, a Noun Card for each noun, and a Blank Card for each word that is neither an article nor a noun.

Look at the first word in the sentence.
• It is one of the three words on the red card.
• Put a red card on your desk to stand for this word.

Look at the second word.
• A boy is a person.
• Look at the clues on the bottom of the white card.
• In this sentence you can say, "Two boys and the girl."
• The word *the* sounds correct in front of the word *boy*. (In fact, the word *the* is already there.)
• Put a white card to the right of the red card to stand for *boy*.

Use a black Blank Card for your third word because:
• It is not *a*, *an*, or *the*.
• It is not a person, place, thing, or idea.
• In this sentence, you cannot put the word *the* in front of the word *and*. You cannot say, "The boy the and the girl."
• In this sentence *two* does not make sense in front of the word *and*.

▬▬▬▬

Continue on, using the clue sides of the cards to discuss each word in the rest of the sentence. The final pattern of cards should look like the arrangement at the top of the next page.

---

*Proper noun exceptions will be discussed later.

Now we will use the sequence of cards to identify parts of speech with symbols (on the overhead or chalkboard).

Possible partial script:

Turn the first card over.
- We see that *the* is an article; therefore, we mark *the* with a check.

Turn the second card over.
- This white card tells us that we have found a noun, so we underline the word *boy.*

Use the reverse sides of the cards in sequence to identify all the words. The model sentence will finally look like this:

      ✓   ✓   ✓   ✓

The <u>boy</u> and the <u>girl</u> saw a <u>man</u> eat an <u>apple</u>.

POSSIBLE PROBLEM

Students may look at the word *saw* and comment, "You can put the word *two* in front of the word *saw*: *two saws.* Doesn't that make *saw* a noun?"

The suggested response to such a comment would be:
- No word is a part of speech unless it appears in context. This means that a word must be used in a sentence before you can say what part of speech it is. Think of the sentence *The boy and the girl saw a man eat an apple.*
- Use the clues at the bottom of the Noun Card: can you say, "The boy and the girl the saw a man."?
- No, that does not make sense, so *saw* is not a noun in the context of this sentence.

Now ask students to return their cards to the proper stacks.

┌─── MEMORY WORK ───────────────────────────────────────┐

At this point students should make sure that they know two rules:
1. No word is a part of speech unless it appears in context.
2. Every article in a sentence means that a noun will follow it, although the noun may not be the very next word.

└──┘

Move on to Worksheet 1.

Students analyze each sentence according to the information on the clue sides of the Noun and Article Cards. Using one card for each word in the sentence, students arrange the cards clue side up in front of them. A Blank Card is used for any word that is neither a noun nor an article.

On their worksheets, students underline each noun and put a check mark over each article in the sentence that corresponds to the one that they have just analyzed using cards. (Students may use the reverse sides of the cards to tell what parts of speech they have identified and to see how to mark these parts of speech on their worksheets.)

The teacher should reinforce important points and circulate around the room, offering help and encouragement.

WORKSHEET

CARDS: Noun, Article, Blank

NEW CONCEPTS: Proper Nouns, Common Nouns

IMPORTANT INFORMATION FOR STUDENTS

- Proper nouns begin with capital letters and name specific persons, places, things, or ideas.
- Multiple-word proper nouns—names like *New York*, titles like *The Wonderful Wizard of Oz*, and dates like *May 18th*—are considered as one noun.
- The clues (the words *the* and *two*) at the bottom of the Noun Card usually do not apply to proper nouns.
- Multiple-word proper nouns should be underlined with one continuous line.
- Nouns that are not capitalized are called common nouns.

Sentence for Practice

Using an overhead projector or a chalkboard, present the following sentence. Analyze this sentence first with cards and then with symbols, using the same procedures as applied in the model lesson for Worksheet 1.

Luis went to San Francisco, and he bought a shirt at Fisherman's Wharf.

Parts of Speech Identified with Clue Cards

Class discussion, led by the teacher, should result in the following pattern of cards:

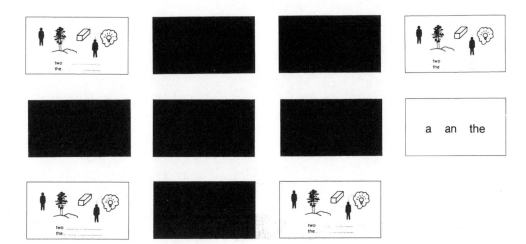

Parts of Speech Identified with Symbols

Class discussion, led by the teacher with the students using their cards, should result in the following:

Luis went to San Francisco, and he bought a shirt at Fisherman's Wharf.

POSSIBLE PROBLEMS

Students may look at the word *he* and comment, "*He* is a person; isn't *he* a noun?".

A suggested response would be:
    Remember the clues at the bottom of the Noun Card? It would make no sense to say, "and the he."

Students may also ask, "Shouldn't there be a $\checkmark$ over *and*?".

A suggested response to this would be:
    If you closely examine the clue side of the Article Card, you will see that you are confusing *and* with *an*.

Move on to Worksheet 2.

On Worksheet 2, students should follow the same steps for analyzing sentences as the ones they used with the teacher in the preceding work: first they analyze a sentence using cards, and then they use symbols to mark articles and nouns on their worksheets.

WORKSHEET

CARDS: Article, Noun, Blank
NEW CONCEPTS: None

Worksheet 3 provides continued practice with articles and nouns, both common and proper.

Teachers may want to add sentences on the board or overhead projector to provide further classwork. When doing so, it's a good idea to copy the surface structure of the sentences on the worksheet. For example, if a worksheet sentence reads *The boy is in the tub*, a teacher's sentence could be *The snake is in the grass*. Otherwise, students may encounter grammatical structures they are not ready to deal with. The sentences in *The Winston Grammar Program* are constructed to avoid such problems. Eliciting sentences from students is not a good idea because a student's oral language is often very complex. Such sentences as *Look, Ma, no hands!* or *Watch me go!* are difficult to analyze even for experts.

Move on to Worksheet 3.

Students shouldn't take shortcuts. They should analyze a sentence with cards on their desks before they use symbols to identify parts of speech on the worksheets. The teacher should remind students to underline multiple-word nouns with one continuous line.

WORKSHEET

CARDS: Article, Noun, Personal Pronoun, Blank
NEW CONCEPT: Personal Pronouns*

Personal Pronoun Card
(Clue Side)

I	we		me	us
you	you		you	you
he	they		him	them
she			her	
it			it	

Personal Pronoun Card
(Reverse Side)

pron.

**personal
pronoun**

S., D.O., I.O., O.P., P.N., App., N.D.A.

IMPORTANT INFORMATION FOR STUDENTS

- Personal pronouns are defined as words (in context) that name persons or things.
- Personal pronouns do not follow articles and do not form plurals by adding *s* as most nouns do.
- All of the personal pronouns are listed on the clue side of the Personal Pronoun Card.
- The reverse side of the card shows that, on the worksheets, personal pronouns should be identified by writing *pron.* over each word that is a personal pronoun.
- The additional information on the reverse side of the Personal Pronoun Card will be discussed later.

Sentences for Practice

To practice application of concepts needed for Worksheet 4, use an overhead projector or a chalkboard to present one or more of the sentences at the top of page 9. Analyze the sentence(s) using what by now should be standard procedure: first use cards and then symbols and abbreviations.

---

*At this point, only personal pronouns are presented. Demonstrative, reflexive, indefinite, and other types of pronouns are brought up in the Advanced Level of this program. These forms of pronouns can be confusing, and it is best to avoid them until students are thoroughly familiar with the other parts of speech.

1. He and I played in the house today.
2. She gave us apples, bananas, and peaches.
3. We will go with him and her.
4. In 1990, they moved to South Dakota.

Sentence 1: Parts of Speech Identified with Clue Cards

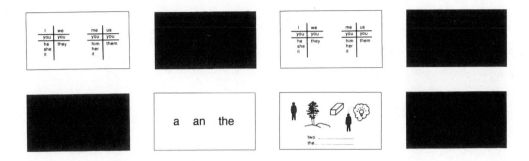

Parts of Speech Identified with Symbols and Abbreviations

1. He and I played in the <u>house</u> today.
   pron.   *pron.*   ✓

2. She gave us <u>apples</u>, <u>bananas</u>, and <u>peaches</u>.
   pron.   *pron.*

3. We will go with <u>him</u> and <u>her</u>.
   pron.   *pron.*   *pron.*

4. In <u>1990</u>, they moved to <u>South Dakota</u>.
       pron.

POSSIBLE PROBLEM

Students may look at the word *today* in sentence *1* and ask, "Isn't *today* a noun?".

Suggested responses would be:
• Can we say, "in the house the today"?
• Does it sound correct to say, "in the house todays"?

Move on to Worksheet 4.

The teacher should remind students that the four piles of cards they will be using should be arranged clue side up. They may cue themselves from the reverse sides of the cards when marking the sentences on their worksheets. At this point, they will be putting a check mark over all articles, underlining all nouns, and writing *pron.* over all personal pronouns.

WORKSHEET

CARDS: Noun, Article, Personal Pronoun, Blank
NEW CONCEPTS: None

In Worksheet 5, students will again identify articles, nouns, and personal pronouns. Before they do this, the teacher should present a thorough review of the parts of speech covered to date. He or she may also want to provide extra sentences for practice. Such sentences should follow the surface structure of the sentences on Worksheet 5.

The teacher should reinforce the two rules that the students memorized for Worksheet 1.

1. No word is a part of speech unless it appears in context.
2. Every article in a sentence means that a noun will follow it.

Move on to Worksheet 5.

As usual, students should use the cards on their desks to analyze each sentence before they analyze it with symbols and abbreviations on the worksheet. The teacher should be active in class to observe students who might be having difficulty.

CARDS: Article, Noun, Personal Pronoun, Verb, Blank
NEW CONCEPT: Verbs

Verb Card
(Clue Side)

Verb Card
(Reverse Side)

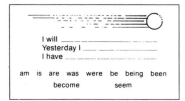

IMPORTANT INFORMATION FOR STUDENTS

- The picture at the top of the clue side of the Verb Card shows a ball in mid-air.
- Underneath the picture of the ball, there are three "lead" phrases. A verb will fit in each blank.

    I will _____

    Yesterday I _____

    I have _____

- If you fill in the blanks with the verb *throw*, you will see the verb form change.*

    I will *throw* the ball.

    Yesterday I *threw* the ball.

    I have *thrown* the ball.

- Many verbs show action.
- Some verbs don't show action. These are *verbs of being* (often called *linking verbs*). The most common verbs of being are listed at the bottom of the clue side of the Verb Card. For now, you should refer to these words simply as *verbs.***
- The reverse side of the Verb Card shows that the symbol for a verb in this program is double underlining.

---

*There are approximately eight verbs in English whose principal parts are identical—they don't change form. These include *cut* and *put*. This program avoids such verbs for the time being.

**Other words can sometimes be linking verbs: It *looks* good. The flowers *smell* sweet. He *waxed* sullen. Such constructions should not be introduced at this time.

Sentence for Practice

Using an overhead projector or the chalkboard, present the following sentence to practice application of concepts needed for Worksheet 6.

Marta speaks to the coach often.

Parts of Speech Identified with Clue Cards

   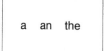

Possible script for explaining the sequence of cards:

Marta is a noun because:
• *Marta* is a person.
• *Marta* is a proper noun because it names a specific person, it is capitalized, and in this sentence you cannot say, "two Martas" or "the Marta."

Speaks is a verb because:
• It shows action.
• It makes sense when used with the clues on the Verb Card. You can say: I will *speak*. Yesterday I *spoke*. I have *spoken*. (The verb changes form in these sentences.)

To is blank because:
• It is not an article, noun, personal pronoun, or verb.

The is an article because:
• It is listed on the clue side of the Article Card.

Coach is a noun because:
• A coach is a person.
• It makes sense to say, "the coach" in this sentence.
• In this sentence, you can say, "two coaches."

Often is blank because:
• It is not an article, noun, personal pronoun, or verb.

Parts of Speech Identified with Symbols and Abbreviations

$$\overset{\checkmark}{}$$

<u>Marta</u> <u><u>speaks</u></u> to the <u>coach</u> often.

If additional practice is needed, use other illustrative sentences.

Move on to Worksheet 6.

The first part of Worksheet 6 gives students some practice in conjugating* a few common verbs. The second part requires the same procedures as the ones required in Worksheets 1-5: card manipulation and transcription of information to the worksheet.

Remind students to:

• Put a check (√) over articles.
• Underline nouns once.
• Put an abbreviation (*pron.*) above personal pronouns.
• Underline verbs twice.
• Leave all other words unmarked.

---

*The term *conjugating* need not be used with the students.

Principal Parts of Some Irregular Verbs

If students have difficulty using the clues on the Verb Card with some irregular verbs, the teacher may want to help the students learn some principal parts. Students need not know the names of the parts; the important thing is for them to learn the verb form for each part and understand how the parts relate to the clues on the Verb Card.

CLUE: I will ___	CLUE: Yesterday I ___	CLUE: I have ___	CLUE: I will ___	CLUE: Yesterday I ___	CLUE: I have ___
beat	beat	beaten	give	gave	given
begin	began	begun	go	went	gone
behold	beheld	beheld	grind	ground	ground
bend	bent	bent	grow	grew	grown
bet	bet	bet	hang	hung, hanged	hung, hanged
bind	bound	bound	have	had	had
bite	bit	bitten	hear	heard	heard
bleed	bled	bled	hide	hid	hidden
break	broke	broken	hit	hit	hit
breed	bred	bred	hold	held	held
bring	brought	brought	hurt	hurt	hurt
build	built	built	keep	kept	kept
burst	burst	burst	know	knew	known
buy	bought	bought	lay	laid	laid
cast	cast	cast	lead	led	led
catch	caught	caught	leave	left	left
choose	chose	chosen	lend	lent	lent
come	came	come	let	let	let
cost	cost	cost	lie	lay	lain
creep	crept	crept	lose	lost	lost
cut	cut	cut	make	made	made
deal	dealt	dealt	mean	meant	meant
dig	dug	dug	meet	met	met
do	did	done	pay	paid	paid
draw	drew	drawn	put	put	put
drink	drank	drunk	rend	rent	rent
drive	drove	driven	rid	rid	rid
eat	ate	eaten	ride	rode	ridden
fall	fell	fallen	ring	rang	rung
feed	fed	fed	rise	rose	risen
feel	felt	felt	run	ran	run
fight	fought	fought	say	said	said
find	found	found	see	saw	seen
flee	fled	fled	seek	sought	sought
fling	flung	flung	sell	sold	sold
fly	flew	flown	send	sent	sent
forget	forgot	forgotten	set	set	set
freeze	froze	frozen	shake	shook	shaken

CLUE: I will ___	CLUE: Yesterday I ___	CLUE: I have ___	CLUE: I will ___	CLUE: Yesterday I ___	CLUE: I have ___
shed	shed	shed ✗	sting	stung	stung
shine	shone	shone	strew	strewed	strewn
shoe	shod ?	shod ?	stride	strode	stridden
shoot	shot	shot	string	strung	strung
show	showed	shown	swear	swore	sworn
shrink	shrank	shrunk	sweep	swept	swept
sing	sang	sung	swim	swam	swum ✗
sink	sank	sunk	swing	swung ✗	swung ✗
sit	sat	sat	take	took	taken
slay	slew ✗	slain ✗	teach	taught	taught
sleep	slept	slept	tear	tore	torn
slide	slid	slid	tell	told	told
sling	slung	slung	think	thought	thought
slink	slunk	slunk	throw	threw	thrown
slit	slit	slit	thrust	thrust	thrust
speak	spoke	spoken	tread	trod	trodden
spend	spent	spent	wear	wore	worn
spin	spun	spun	weave	wove	woven
split	split	split	weep	wept	wept
spread	spread	spread	wet	wet	wet
spring	sprang	sprung	win	won	won
stand	stood	stood	wind	wound	wound
steal	stole	stolen	wring	wrung	wrung
stick	stuck	stuck	write	wrote	written

16

WORKSHEET

CARDS: Article, Noun, Personal Pronoun, Verb, Blank
NEW CONCEPTS: None

Worksheet 7 provides more practice on the concepts covered in Worksheets 1-6.

Move on to Worksheet 7.

Students shouldn't take shortcuts. They should follow the established procedures of first analyzing a sentence with clue cards and then with symbols and abbreviations on the worksheet. The teacher should circulate among students identifying those who may be having difficulty.

Quiz

After completing Worksheet 7, the teacher should give students Quiz 1. Students may be allowed to use the small clue cards if needed.

WORKSHEET

CARDS: Article, Noun, Personal Pronoun, Verb, Helping Verb, Blank

NEW CONCEPT: Helping Verbs

Helping Verb Card
(Clue Side)

| may / might / must |
| shall / should |
| will / would |
| can / could |
| has / have / had |
| do / did / does |

Helping Verb Card
(Reverse Side)

helping verb

⌐──IMPORTANT INFORMATION FOR STUDENTS──

⚹• A helping verb appears before the main verb.
• Helping verbs are listed on the clue side of the Helping Verb Card.
• Some verbs can be either helping verbs or being verbs (linking verbs). Such words are listed at the bottom of the clue side of the Verb Card.*
• The reverse side of the Helping Verb Card shows that the symbol for a helping verb is double underlining.

Sentence for Practice

Using an overhead projector or a chalkboard, present the following sentence to practice application of concepts needed for Worksheet 8.

The teacher and I have worked hard.

---

*Since the symbol system used on the worksheets in *The Winston Grammar Program* does not distinguish helping verbs from being verbs (linking verbs) or action verbs, elaborate differentiation for students is not yet necessary. (Later, when students are determining noun functions, they will need to be able to identify the main verb and distinguish between action verbs and linking verbs.)

Parts of Speech Identified with Clue Cards

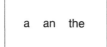   

Parts of Speech Identified with Symbols and Abbreviations

The <u>teacher</u> and I ✓ <u>have</u> <u>worked</u> hard.
                    pron.

Additional Sentence to Analyze*

(first with clue cards; then with symbols and abbreviations)

The <u>job</u> <u>may</u> not <u>seem</u> easy to you.
                                    pron.

Move on to Worksheet 8.

Students should use the standard procedures for card manipulation and analysis of sentences on the worksheets.

---

*Occasionally, directions will provide additional sentences to analyze. Such sentences give students an opportunity to work with the more difficult kinds of examples that may appear on the upcoming worksheet.

WORKSHEET

CARDS: Article, Noun, Personal Pronoun, Verb, Helping Verb, Blank

NEW CONCEPT: Contractions

IMPORTANT INFORMATION FOR STUDENTS

- Contractions contain two parts of speech in one word.*
- Contractions often combine a pronoun with a linking verb or a helping verb.

  Example: You're = You are

  She'll = She will

- Put two cards in one space (one on top of the other) to indicate the two parts of speech in a contraction.

  Example: You're   She'll

Sentence for Practice

Using an overhead projector or the chalkboard, present the following sentence to practice application of concepts needed for Worksheet 9.

I'm unhappy about the game.

---

*Many contractions involve the word *not*. Such contractions should be avoided for now; they will be discussed later. Teachers may want to give students some practice forming contractions.

Parts of Speech Identified with Clue Cards

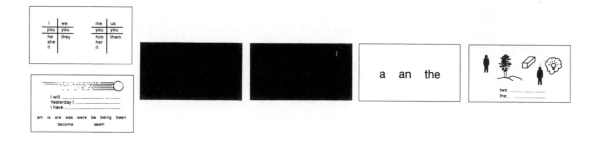

Parts of Speech Identified with Symbols and Abbreviations

pron.

I'm unhappy about the game.

Additional Sentence to Analyze

(first with clue cards; then with symbols and abbreviations)

pron.

They've seen the movie.

Move on to Worksheet 9.

Follow the usual procedures. Remind students to put two cards in one space (one on top of the other) to indicate the two parts of speech in a contraction.

CARDS: Article, Noun, Personal Pronoun, Verb, Helping
        Verb, Blank

NEW CONCEPT: Interrogative Sentences

IMPORTANT INFORMATION FOR STUDENTS

- An interrogative sentence asks a question.
- A sentence that asks a question separates the helping verb from the main verb.

  Example: Did Sam McCall go into the store on an errand?
              (*Did* is the helping verb, and *go* is the main verb.)

- The best way to analyze a sentence that asks a question is to rearrange the words (perhaps only mentally) to make a statement. Rearrangement makes it easier to find verbs.*

  Example: Sam McCall did go into the store on an errand.

Parts of Speech Identified with Clue Cards

(for the interrogative version of the sentence)

---

*It also makes it easier later to find subjects.

Parts of Speech Identified with Symbols and Abbreviations

Did Sam McCall go into the store on an errand?

Additional Sentences to Analyze
(first with clue cards; then with symbols and abbreviations)

Is San Diego located in California?

Did the girl say she'd like a hamburger?

Move on to Worksheet 10.

Follow the usual procedures.

CARDS: Article, Noun, Personal Pronoun, Verb, Helping
Verb, Adjective, Blank
NEW CONCEPT: Adjectives

Adjective Card
(Clue Side)

Adjective Card
(Reverse Side)

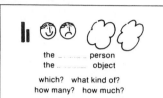

Before students work with the orange Adjective Card, they should use markers
to color the two figures in the upper right-hand corner of the card. Each figure
should be a different color to create the clue that words that name colors are often
adjectives.

- Adjectives are words like *big, small; tall, short; happy, sad; friendly, unfriendly; dark, light.* As these pairs of words show, many adjectives have antonyms.
- The clues in the middle of the adjective card show that an adjective will often make sense between the article *the* and a noun (a person or an object).

   Examples: the *happy* boy   the *sad* boy
               the *clean* glass   the *dirty* glass

- Many adjectives will also make sense between the articles *a* or *an* and nouns that are places as well as nouns that are persons or objects.

   Example: a *new* stadium   an *old* stadium.

- Many adjectives are found directly to the left of a noun, but this is not always the case. Adjectives are often found to the right of a linking verb.

   Example: The present is *big*, but the box is *small.*

- The clues at the bottom of the card show common questions that adjectives answer.

   Examples: Which wagon?   the *red** wagon
               What kind of computer?   a *personal* computer
               How many antelopes?   *three* antelopes

- Many adjectives have more than one form:
   the *heavy* suitcase
   the *heavier* suitcase
   the *heaviest* suitcase
- The reverse side of the Adjective Card shows that, on worksheets, adjectives should be identified by writing *adj.* over each word that is an adjective.
- The additional information on the reverse side of the Adjective Card will be discussed later.

Sentence for Practice

Using an overhead projector or the chalkboard, present the following sentence to practice application of concepts needed for Worksheet 11.

   A familiar face appeared on the movie screen.

---

*Colors can, of course, be nouns in sentences such as *I like the red in the picture.* The rules concerning plurals and articles should lead students to identify *red* as a noun in this context. In the sentence *I like the red paint in the picture*, red* is an adjective. You cannot say, "reds paint."

Parts of Speech Identified with Clue Cards

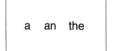  

Possible script for explaining the sequence of cards:

A is an article because:
• It appears on the Article Card.

Familiar is an adjective because:
• It makes sense between an article and a noun (a *familiar* face).
• It answers the question "*What kind of* face?".
• It has an antonym (*unfamiliar*).

Face is a noun because:
• A face is a thing.
• It follows an article (*a*).
• Saying "two faces" makes sense.

Appeared is a verb because:
• It shows action.
• It fits into the second blank on the Verb Card: (Yesterday I *appeared*).

On is blank because:
• It isn't any part of speech learned so far.

The is an article because:
• It appears on the Article Card.

Movie is an adjective because:
• It makes sense between an article and a noun (the *movie* screen).
• It answers the question "*Which* screen?".

Screen is a noun because:
• A screen is a thing.
• It makes sense to say, "two screens."
• It makes sense when it follows the word *the*.

┌─**POSSIBLE PROBLEM**─────────────────────────────────┐

Students may look at the word *movie* and say, "Isn't *movie* a noun?".

Suggested responses to such a comment would be:
• No word is a part of speech until it appears in context.
• Use the clues at the bottom of the Noun Card. Does "the movies screen" make sense? Remember, in order to pass the "clue" test, a noun must be able to take a plural form in the context of the sentence at hand.

└──┘

Parts of Speech Identified with Symbols and Abbreviations

    √ *adj.*   √ *adj.*
A familiar <u>face</u> <u>appeared</u> on the movie <u>screen</u>.

Additional Sentences to Analyze

  √ *adj.*   √ *adj.*
The big <u>tree</u> in the front <u>yard</u> <u>fell</u> yesterday.

  √   √   *adj.*
The <u>train</u> in the <u>museum</u> <u>is</u> old.

pron. √ *adj.*   √   *adj.*
I'd <u>like</u> a ripe <u>apple</u> and a <u>slice</u> of cheddar <u>cheese</u>.

Move on to Worksheet 11.

Follow the usual procedures.

WORKSHEET

CARDS: Article, Noun, Personal Pronoun, Verb, Helping
Verb, Adjective, Adverb, Blank
NEW CONCEPT: Adverbs

Adverb Card
(Clue Side)

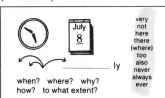

Adverb Card
(Reverse Side)

- Illustrations at the top left side of the Adverb Card show three important facts about adverbs:

  Adverbs often deal with time (shown by the clock and the calendar).

  Adverbs often can be moved to another place in the sentence (shown by the arrows).

  Adverbs often end in *ly*, although not all *ly* words are adverbs.

- Adverbs often answer the following questions listed at the bottom of the clue card:

  When?

  How?

  Where?

  To what extent?

  Why?

- The words at the right side of the clue card should be labeled as adverbs.*
- The adverb *not* is often contained in a contraction.

  Example: Isn't

  CARDS**   SYMBOLS AND
                             ABBREVIATIONS

  adv.
  isn't

- *Won't* is a contraction for *will not*.
- The reverse side of the adverb card shows that, on worksheets, adverbs should be identified by writing *adv.* over each word that is an adverb.
- The additional information on the reverse side of the Adverb Card will be discussed later.

---

*Some of these words can be other parts of speech, but such constructions are avoided in the exercises for now. *Where* is in parentheses because it can be "tricky" to deal with. Teachers should stress that *not* and *very* are always adverbs.

**Teachers may need to remind students to put two cards in one space (one on top of the other) to show the two parts of speech in a contraction.

Sentence for Practice

Using an overhead projector or a chalkboard, present the following sentence to practice application of concepts needed for Worksheet 12.

Unfortunately, I can't come to the party tonight.

Parts of Speech Identified with Clue Cards

 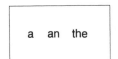 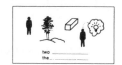 

Possible script for explaining the sequence of cards:

Unfortunately is an adverb because:
- It ends in *ly*.
- It can be moved to another place in the sentence (*I can't come to the party tonight, unfortunately*).

I is a personal pronoun because:
- *I* appears on the Personal Pronoun Card.

Can't is a contraction because:
- It is one word made from two different parts of speech—the helping verb *can* and the adverb *not*.

Come is a verb because:
- It shows action.
- It can be used with the clues on the Verb Card.
  You can say: I will *come*.   Yesterday I *came*.   I have *come*.

To is blank because:
- It is none of the parts of speech learned so far.

The is an article because:
- It is listed on the clue side of the Article Card.

Party is a noun because:
• It is a place.
• It follows the article *the*.
• It makes sense to say, "two parties."

Tonight is an adverb because:
• It deals with time. (It answers the question *When?*)
• It can be moved to another point in the sentence.

Parts of Speech Identified with Symbols and Abbreviations

adv. pron. adv.   ✓ adv.
Unfortunately, I can't come to the party tonight.

Additional Sentences to Analyze

1. Won't you go home for the holiday?*
2. Yesterday we went to the concert.
3. The car will slowly climb the hill.**

---

*This sentence gives students practice with a contraction in an interrogative sentence. It also presents students with *home* used as an adverb rather than as a noun. They should see that *home* in this context answers the question "*Where?*" They should also understand that the clues at the bottom of the Noun Card do not work with *home* in this sentence.

**Before beginning the worksheets, students may need to see how some adverbs can be moved within a sentence: *Slowly the car will climb the hill* or *The car will climb the hill slowly*. This sentence is also good for illustrating the fact that an adverb sometimes appears between the helping verb and the main verb.

Sentence 1: Parts of Speech Identified with Clue Cards

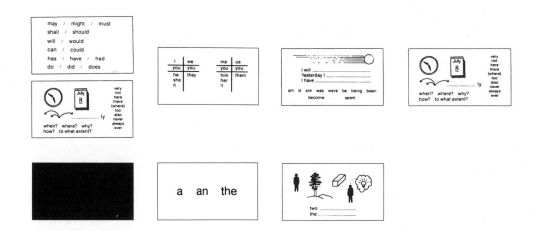

Parts of Speech Identified with Symbols and Abbreviations

1. Won't you go home for the holiday?

2. Yesterday we went to the concert.

3. The car will slowly climb the hill.

Move on to Worksheet 12.

Students should follow the usual procedures.

WORKSHEET

CARDS: Article, Noun, Personal Pronoun, Verb, Helping
Verb, Adjective, Adverb, Blank

NEW CONCEPTS: None

Worksheet 13 provides students with more practice on identifying parts of speech, particularly adverbs and adjectives.

Remind students that no word is a part of speech unless it appears in context.

Move on to Worksheet 13.

Students should continue to use the cards to analyze sentences presented on the worksheet before they use symbols and abbreviations to mark the worksheet.

Quiz

After completing Worksheet 13, students should be ready to take Quiz 2 using the clue cards if needed.

CARDS: Article, Noun, Personal Pronoun, Verb, Helping
Verb, Adjective, Adverb, Blank

NEW CONCEPT: Modification

Adjective Card
(Clue Side)

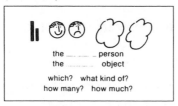

the _____ person
the _____ object

which?   what kind of?
how many?   how much?

Adjective Card
(Reverse Side)

adj.
adjective   noun /
pronoun

Adverb Card
(Clue Side)

_____ ly

when?   where?   why?
how?   to what extent?

very
not
here
there
(where)
too
also
never
always
ever

Adverb Card
(Reverse Side)

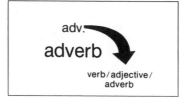

adv.
adverb

verb / adjective /
adverb

- The reverse side of the Adjective Card shows that adjectives modify or describe nouns or pronouns. It also shows that an arrow should be drawn from the adjective to the noun or pronoun that it modifies.
- Adjectives modify nouns or pronouns by answering questions like:
     Which?
     What kind of?
     How many?
     How much?
  These questions are listed on the clue side of the Adjective Card.
- The reverse side of the Adverb Card shows that adverbs modify or describe verbs, adjectives, or other adverbs and that an arrow should be drawn from the adverb to the word it modifies.
- The clue side of the Adverb Card shows that adverbs often answer the following questions:
     When?
     How?
     Where?
     To what extent?
     Why?
- The adverbs *not* and *very* almost always modify the words right next to them.

Sentence for Practice

Use an overhead projector or the chalkboard to explain the following example.

He rose slowly from the back seat.

Parts of Speech Analyzed with Clue Cards

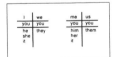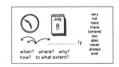

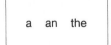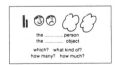

Sentence Analyzed with Symbols and Abbreviations

pron.   *—adv.*   ✓ *adj—*
He <u>rose</u> slowly from the back <u>seat</u>.

Possible partial script:

Slowly is an adverb because:
- It ends in *ly*.
- It can be moved to another part of the sentence.
- It answers the question "Rose *how*?" "Rose *slowly*." In other words, it modifies the verb *rose*.

Back is an adjective because:
- It makes sense between an article and a noun (the *back* seat).
- It answers the question "*Which* seat?" "The *back* seat." In other words, it modifies the noun *seat*.

Additional Sentences to Analyze

✓ *adj.*   *—adv. adv.—* *adj*
The tan <u>puppy</u> <u>wasn't</u> very frisky.

pron.   ✓   *adv.—adv.*
I <u>found</u> the <u>key</u> right here.

✓ *adj.*   *adv.*   ✓ *adj.*
The black <u>cat</u> closely <u>watched</u> the little <u>mouse</u>.

✓ *adj.*   *adv.—adv.*   ✓
The dark <u>clouds</u> <u>gathered</u> rather quickly before the <u>storm</u>.

If students have trouble differentiating between adjectives and adverbs, tell them that adjectives usually cannot be moved around within a sentence. Adverbs often can be moved around, but when they are, the other words in the sentence must remain in sequence.

Move on to Worksheet 14.

WORKSHEET

CARDS: Article, Noun, Personal Pronoun, Verb, Helping
Verb, Adjective, Adverb, Preposition, Blank

NEW CONCEPT: Prepositions

Preposition Card
(Clue Side)

Preposition Card
(Reverse Side)

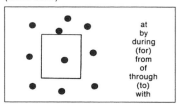

prep.

(preposition

IMPORTANT INFORMATION FOR STUDENTS

- The box and the dots on the clue side of the Preposition Card show that many prepositions indicate location.

  Examples: in on over across beneath beside above under
  along toward up among around near between
  behind below

- The list on the right side of the clue card names some words that are almost always prepositions although they do not show location. *For* and *to* are often other parts of speech, so they are placed in parentheses.

- Some common prepositions do not indicate location and are not listed on the right side of the Preposition Card.

  Examples: about after against before down except off until

- The reverse side of the Preposition Card shows that students should label a preposition by writing *prep.* above it and, at this point, by placing an initial parenthesis before it.

Sentence for Practice

Present the following sentence to illustrate the concepts needed for Worksheet 15.

The broad river flows gently under the bridge.

Parts of Speech Identified with Clue Cards

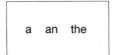  

 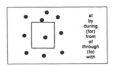 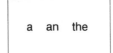 

Possible script:

The is an article because:
- *The* appears on the article card.

Broad is an adjective because:
- *Broad* makes sense between an article and a noun.
- It has an antonym (*narrow*).
- It modifies the noun *river*. It answers the question "*Which* river?" or "*What kind of* river?".

River is a noun because:
- You can say, "the river" or "two rivers."

Flows is a verb because:
- It shows action.
- It makes sense when used with the clues on the verb card. You can say: It will *flow*. Yesterday it *flowed*. It has *flowed*. (The verb changes form in the sentences above.)

Gently is an adverb because:
- It ends in *ly*.
- It can be moved within the sentence.
- *Gently* modifies the verb *flows* and answers the question "How?".

Under is a preposition because:
- It is a word that shows location.

The is an article because:
- *The* appears on the Article Card.

Bridge is a noun because:
- It is a thing.
- It makes sense to say, "the bridge" or "two bridges."

Sentence Analyzed with Symbols and Abbreviations

The broad river flows gently under the bridge.

(analysis markings: ✓ adj.→ over "river"; adv.← over "flows"; prep. and ✓ over "under...bridge"; "river," "flows," and "bridge" underlined)

MEMORY WORK

It will help students to memorize the following:
• Many prepositions are words that indicate location.
• Some common prepositions do not indicate location (and are not listed on the right side of the Preposition Card).

Examples: about   after   against   before   down   except   off   until

---

Move on to Worksheet 15.

WORKSHEET

CARDS: Article, Noun, Personal Pronoun, Verb, Helping Verb, Adjective, Adverb, Preposition, Blank

NEW CONCEPT: Prepositional Phrases

IMPORTANT INFORMATION FOR STUDENTS

- A prepositional phrase is a group of words that begins with a preposition and ends with a noun or a pronoun.
- The noun or pronoun at the end of the prepositional phrase is called the object of the preposition.
- The object of a preposition will answer the question "Whom?" or "What?".
- The object of a preposition is labeled O.P.
- A prepositional phrase is placed within parentheses.
- A prepositional phrase can act as an adjective modifying a noun or a pronoun or as an adverb modifying a verb (or sometimes an adjective or another adverb).*
- Students should write the letters ADJ. or ADV. over a prepositional phrase and draw an arrow to the word it modifies.

Example: the girl in the booth

In is a preposition because it is a word that shows location like the words *on, under, over, beside.*

Booth is a noun, and it answers the question "In *what*?". Therefore, *booth* is the object of the preposition.

The prepositional phrase *in the booth* acts as an adjective because it modifies the noun *girl*. It answers the question "*Which* girl?".

$$\text{the } \underline{\text{girl}} \left(\underline{\text{in}} \text{ the } \underline{\text{booth}} \right)$$

---

*Teachers may also want to point out to students that, like single-word adverbs, prepositional phrases acting as adverbs usually can be moved to another place in the sentence and still make sense. Another piece of information that may be helpful is that a prepositional phrase acting as an adjective usually follows the noun or pronoun that it modifies.

Sentence for Practice

Present the following sentence to practice application of concepts needed for Worksheet 16.

The girl in the booth hasn't worked very long.

Parts of Speech Analyzed with Clue Cards

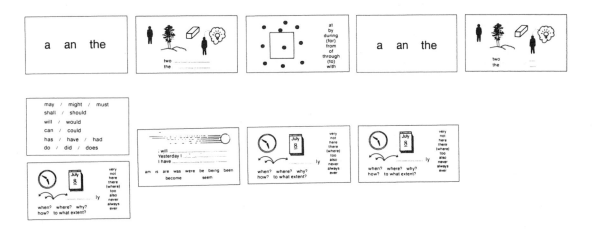

Sentence Analyzed with Symbols and Abbreviations

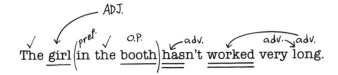

Additional Sentences to Analyze

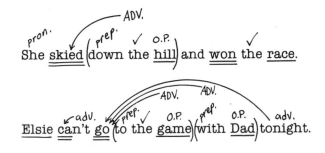

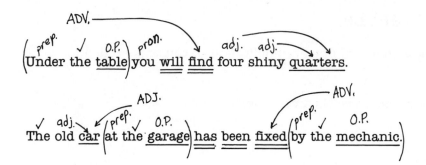

The old car (at the garage) has been fixed (by the mechanic.)

Move on to Worksheet 16.

CARDS: Article, Noun, Personal Pronoun, Verb, Helping
Verb, Adjective, Adverb, Preposition, Blank
NEW CONCEPTS: None

Worksheet 17 provides additional practice in identifying all parts of speech covered to date, words modified, objects of prepositions, and prepositional phrases.

The teacher may wish to prepare students for this review by presenting the following sentences. The first is particularly useful for illustrating an *ly* word that is not an adverb.

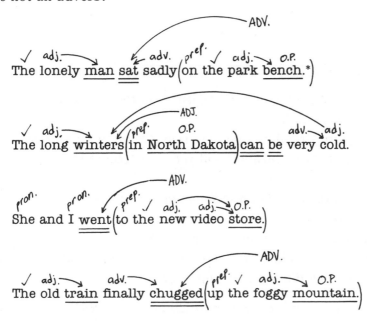

Move on to Worksheet 17.

---

*The students should see that *lonely* is an adjective modifying a noun. It cannot be moved to another part of the sentence the way an adverb can. Also, it answers an adjective question "*Which* man?" or "*What kind of* man?".

WORKSHEET

CARDS: Article, Noun, Personal Pronoun, Verb, Helping Verb, Adjective, Adverb, Preposition, Coordinating Conjunction, Blank

NEW CONCEPT: Coordinating Conjunctions

Coordinating Conjunction Card
(Clue Side)

Coordinating Conjunction Card
(Reverse Side)

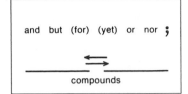

┌─IMPORTANT INFORMATION FOR STUDENTS─┐

- Six words that are coordinating conjunctions are listed on the clue side of the Coordinating Conjunction Card.
- *For* and *yet* are placed within parentheses because they are often mislabeled. (For example, *for* is sometimes a preposition and *yet* is sometimes an adverb.)
- A semicolon (;) is shown on the card because sometimes it can be used instead of a coordinating conjunction.
- The arrows and the lines below the list on the card show that compounds are two equal grammatical units linked by a coordinating conjunction.
- A grammatical unit is a word, a phrase, or a sentence.

  Examples of grammatical units linked by coordinating conjunctions:
    Words: *Liza* or *Franco*
    Phrases: *Over the river* and *through the woods*
    Sentences: *I'm here,* but *you're there.*

- Whatever grammatical unit appears to the left of the coordinating conjunction must also appear somewhere to the right of the conjunction.
- The reverse side of the Coordinating Conjunction Card shows that the symbol for this part of speech is *c.c.*

44

Sentence for Practice

Present the following sentence to practice application of concepts needed for Worksheet 18.

Stanley and Anita Terpak have three daughters in college.

Parts of Speech Analyzed with Clue Cards

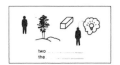   

 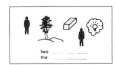 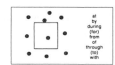 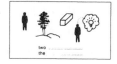

Sentence Analyzed with Symbols and Abbreviations

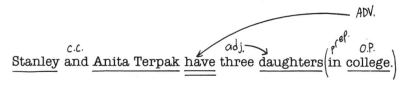

And is a coordinating conjunction because:
- It is on the clue side of the Coordinating Conjunction Card.
- It links two similar grammatical units, one to its left and one to its right.
- The grammatical units linked by the coordinating conjunction are words: *Stanley* and *Anita Terpak*.

Additional Sentences to Analyze

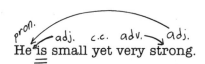

Yet is a coordinating conjunction linking two grammatical units that are words: *small* yet *strong*.

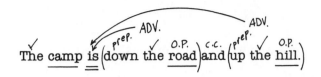

The camp is (down the road) and (up the hill.)

And is a coordinating conjunction linking two grammatical units that are phrases: *down the road* and *up the hill.*

---MEMORY WORK---

At this point, students should memorize the following:
- The coordinating conjunctions are *and, but, or, nor,* and sometimes *for* and *yet.*
- The semicolon (;) is often used in place of a coordinating conjunction.
- Coordinating conjunctions form compounds. A compound is made up of two similar grammatical units.
- A unit may be a word, a phrase, or a sentence.
- The same kind of grammatical unit will appear on both the left and the right of the coordinating conjunction in a compound.

Move on to Worksheet 18.

WORKSHEET

19

CARDS: Article, Noun, Personal Pronoun, Verb, Helping Verb, Adjective, Adverb, Preposition, Coordinating Conjunction, Blank

NEW CONCEPTS: None

Worksheet 19 provides additional practice on identifying all parts of speech covered to date, objects of prepositions, prepositional phrases, and words modified.

Before students begin Worksheet 19, the teacher may want to review the material that should have been memorized up to this point:

• No word is a part of speech unless it appears in context.

• Every article in a sentence means that a noun will follow it.

• Many prepositions indicate location. Some that do not indicate location and that are not listed on the right side of the Preposition Card are *about, after, against, before, down, except, off, until.*

• The coordinating conjunctions are *and, but, or, nor,* and sometimes *for* and *yet.* A semicolon is sometimes used instead of a coordinating conjunction.

• Coordinating conjunctions link two similar grammatical units such as words, phrases, or sentences.

Move on to Worksheet 19.

WORKSHEET

CARDS: Article, Noun, Personal Pronoun, Verb, Helping Verb, Adjective, Adverb, Preposition, Coordinating Conjunction, Interjection*

NEW CONCEPT: Interjections

Interjection Card
(Clue Side)

Interjection Card
(Reverse Side)

IMPORTANT INFORMATION FOR STUDENTS

- The clue side of the Interjection Card shows that interjections are words that indicate noise, emotion or speed.

  Examples: Ouch! Wow! Zap! Boom! Zip! Whoosh!

- The reverse side of the Interjection Card shows that the symbol for an interjection is an exclamation point (!).

Sentence for Practice

Wow, Tom, you've lost ten pounds!

---

*Worksheet 20 introduces the last of the Clue Cards. From this point on, students will not need a blank card for the sentences presented in the Basic Level of *The Winston Grammar Program.*

Parts of Speech Analyzed with Clue Cards

 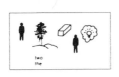 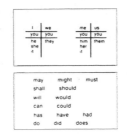 

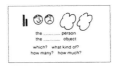 

Sentence Analyzed with Symbols and Abbreviations

Wow, Tom, you've lost ten pounds!

Move on to Worksheet 20.

WORKSHEET

CARDS: All cards except the blank card
NEW CONCEPTS: None

Worksheet 21 provides practice on all concepts covered to date: parts of speech, modification, prepositional phrases.

Move on to Worksheet 21.

Quiz

After completing Worksheet 21, students should be ready to take Quiz 3 using the clue cards if needed.

WORKSHEET

CARDS: All cards except the blank card
NEW CONCEPT: The Ellipsis

IMPORTANT INFORMATION FOR STUDENTS

- An ellipsis is **any** part of a sentence that is not directly expressed (not put into words) but that is necessary to make a sentence grammatically complete.

  Example: Go to first base really means *You go to first base.*

  Omitting the word *you* in the first sentence creates the ellipsis.

  Other examples with elliptical words in parentheses:
  1. *Thank you for the lovely flowers.*
     or
     (I) thank you for the lovely flowers.

  2. *I know she is here.*
     or
     I know (that) she is here.

  3. *She is taller than he.*
     or
     She is taller than he (is tall).

- If the omission of a pronoun creates an ellipsis, show this by using the personal pronoun card. On the worksheet the omitted personal pronoun should be added and placed within parentheses as in the examples.

Sentence for Practice

Get the papers from the desk.

Parts of Speech Analyzed with Clue Cards

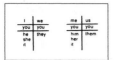  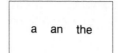 

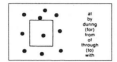 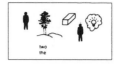 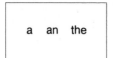

Sentence Analyzed with Symbols and Abbreviations

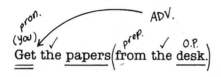

Move on to Worksheet 22.

CARDS: All Parts of Speech Cards
Noun Function Card 1
NEW CONCEPT: Subjects

Noun Function Card 1

1

FINDING THE SUBJECT

Look at the main verb in your sentence.
Say, "WHO or WHAT;" then quickly read
the verb. The answer is the subject.
Mark it with an S.

Ex: The dog bit the girl.

"WHO or WHAT bit?"

The dog bit; dog is the subject.

The dog bit the girl.

Find the subject for each main verb in the
sentence.

GO TO CARD #2 (BLUE).

Sentence for Practice

Arnold Goya came through the front door.

Sentence Analyzed with Clue Cards

  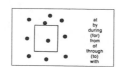

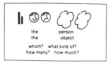 

Sentence Analyzed with Symbols and Abbreviations

Use Noun Function Card 1 to find the subject after all parts of speech have been identified.

S.   ADV.
              prep.   ✓ adj. O.P.
Arnold Goya came (through the front door.)

Additional Sentences to Analyze

S.   S.
pron. c.c. pron.   ✓   adv.
He and she enjoyed the movie tonight.

S.   S.
pron.   ✓   c.c. pron.   ✓
I rang the bell, and he answered the door.

S.
pron   pron. ✓
Are you asking me a question?

ADV.   ADJ.
prep. ✓ O.P. S. pron.   ✓   prep. O.P.
(Inside the box,) you'll find a letter (from Aunt Betty.)

MEMORY WORK

Students should memorize:
- All nouns and pronouns in a sentence perform a noun function.
- The subject of a sentence is never found inside a prepositional phrase.

Move on to Worksheet 23.

CARDS: All Parts of Speech Cards
        Noun Function Cards 1 and 2*
NEW CONCEPTS: Action and Linking Verbs

Noun Function Card 2

2

**IS THE MAIN VERB AN <u>ACTION</u>
<u>VERB</u> OR A <u>LINKING VERB</u>?**

The common linking verbs are:

am	be
is	being
are	been
was	seem
were	become

If the verb is a <u>linking verb</u>,
       GO TO CARD #5 (GREEN).

If the verb is an <u>action verb</u>,
       GO TO CARD #3 (YELLOW).

IMPORTANT INFORMATION FOR STUDENTS

- There are two kinds of verbs—action verbs and linking verbs (sometimes called *being* verbs).
- Common linking verbs appear on Noun Function Card 2.
- Any main verb not on this card is an action verb.
- If a helping verb is present, the verb that follows it is the main verb.

Sentence for Practice

I don't like cold pizza.

---

*Noun Function Cards should be used after all parts of speech have been identified.

Sentence Analyzed with Clue Cards

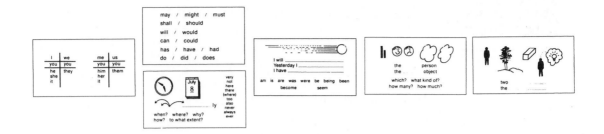

Sentence Analyzed with Symbols and Abbreviations

Use Noun Function Card 1 to find the subject.

Use Noun Function Card 2 to decide whether the verb is an action verb or a linking verb.

S.
pron.   adv.   adj.
I don't like cold pizza.

Like is the main verb. Since it does not appear on Noun Function Card 2, it is an action verb.

Move on to Worksheet 24.

WORKSHEET

25

CARDS: All Parts of Speech Cards
Noun Function Cards 1, 2, 3
NEW CONCEPT: Direct Objects

Noun Function Card 3

> ## 3
> **FINDING THE DIRECT OBJECT**
> You have decided that the main verb is
> an action verb. The sentence <u>may</u> have a
> direct object.
> Read the subject and verb in the sentence;
> then say, "WHOM or WHAT?"
> The answer is the direct object. Circle it.
>
> Ex: The <u>dog</u> <u>bit</u> the <u>girl</u>.
>
> "The dog bit <u>whom or what</u>?"
>
> The dog bit the <u>girl</u>; <u>girl</u> is the direct object.
>
> The <u>dog</u> <u>bit</u> the (girl.)
>
> Not all action verbs have direct objects.
>
> The <u>game</u> <u>has started</u>.
>
> Try to find a direct object for each <u>action</u> verb
> in the sentence. After you find the
> direct object(s),
>   GO TO CARD #4 (ORANGE).
> If there is no direct object in the sentence,
>   GO TO CARD #6 (TAN).

══ IMPORTANT INFORMATION FOR STUDENTS ══

- After an action verb, there may be a direct object.
- A direct object does not follow a linking verb.
- A direct object must be a noun or a pronoun.
- Noun Function Card 3 shows how to find the direct object:
    Read the subject and the verb.
    Then ask "Whom?" or "What?".
    The answer is the direct object.

Example: She gave me a dime.

The subject and verb are *She gave*. She gave *what?* She gave *dime*. *Dime* is the direct object.

- The symbol for a direct object is a circle around a word.

58

Sentence for Practice

The pitcher took signals from the catcher.

Sentence Analyzed with Clue Cards

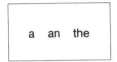  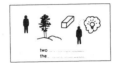 

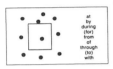 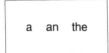 

Sentence Analyzed with Symbols and Abbreviations

Use Noun Function Card 1 to find the subject.
Use Noun Function Card 2 to decide whether the verb is action or linking.
Use Noun Function Card 3 to find the direct object.

Additional Sentence to Analyze

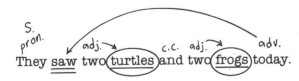

Move on to Worksheet 25.

CARDS: All Parts of Speech Cards
Noun Function Cards 1-4
NEW CONCEPT: Indirect Objects

Noun Function Card 4

4

FINDING THE INDIRECT OBJECT

If a sentence has an action verb <u>and</u> a direct
object, it <u>MAY</u> have an indirect object.
Is there a noun or pronoun between the
action verb and the direct object? If not,

GO TO CARD #6 (TAN).

If there is, it <u>MAY</u> be an indirect object.
Put the words <u>to</u> or <u>for</u> in front of this noun or
pronoun. Move it to the right of the direct
object. Read the sentence. Does it make
sense? If it makes sense, that noun or
pronoun is an <u>indirect object</u>. Put a box
around it.

Ex: I gave her a ring.

Is there a noun or pronoun between the action
verb and the direct object? (Yes, <u>her</u>)

Can you put <u>to</u> or <u>for</u> in front of it and move it
to the right of the direct object?

(I gave a ring <u>to</u> her.)

Her is the indirect object.
Put a box around it.

I gave [her] a ring.

GO TO CARD #6 (TAN).

IMPORTANT INFORMATION FOR STUDENTS

- An indirect object is a noun or a pronoun that comes between an action verb and a direct object.
- An indirect object can be moved to the right of the direct object if the word *to* or the word *for* is placed in front of it.

  Example: She gave him a puppy.

  She gave a puppy to him.

  They will give us a party.

  They will give a party for us.

- The symbol for an indirect object is a box around a word.

Sentence for Practice

Aunt Emily sent me a postcard from Brazil.

Sentence Analyzed with Clue Cards

   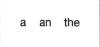

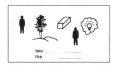 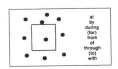 

Sentence Analyzed with Symbols and Abbreviations

Use Noun Function Cards 1, 2, 3, and 4 to:
- find the subject;
- determine whether the verb is action or linking;
- find the direct object;
- find the indirect object.

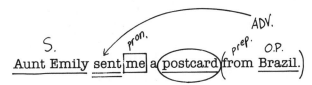

MEMORY WORK

Students should memorize:
- A sentence cannot contain an indirect object unless it contains a direct object.
- Each noun or pronoun performs only one noun function.

Move on to Worksheet 26.

CARDS: All Parts of Speech Cards
       Noun Function Cards 1-5
NEW CONCEPT: Predicate Nominatives*

Noun Function Card 5

5

**FINDING A
PREDICATE NOMINATIVE**

Is there a noun or pronoun after the linking verb in
the sentence? Does this noun or pronoun name
the same thing or person as the subject? If it does,
it is a predicate nominative. Mark it P.N.

Ex: Bob is a good dancer.

Is there a noun after the linking verb?
Yes, dancer. Is Bob the dancer? Is the dancer the
same person as Bob? YES

Bob is a good dancer.

Not all linking verbs have predicate
nominatives.

Ex: He is (in the Navy.)

Try to find a predicate nominative for each
linking verb.

GO TO CARD #6 (TAN).

---

*The Winston Grammar Program uses the term *predicate nominative* rather than *predicate noun* for two
reasons:
1) Predicate "nouns" often are not nouns—they are pronouns. Use of the term *predicate noun*, therefore,
   can be confusing to students.
2) *I*, *he*, *we*, *she*, and *they* are nominative pronouns. Using the term *predicate nominative* will facilitate
   students' understanding of why we use nominative case pronouns in constructions like *It was she*.

- A predicate nominative is a noun or a pronoun that follows a linking verb.
- A predicate nominative names the same person, place, thing, or idea as the subject.

   Example: Jenny was the winner yesterday.

- *Winner* is a noun following a linking verb. *Winner* and *Jenny* name the same person.
- The abbreviation for predicate nominative is *P.N.*

Sentence for Practice

He is the leader of the band.

Sentence Analyzed with Clue Cards

  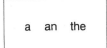 

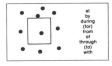 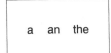 

Sentence Analyzed with Symbols and Abbreviations

Use Noun Function Cards 1-5 to:
- find the subject;
- determine whether the verb is action or linking;
- find the direct object, if there is one;
- find the indirect object, if there is one;
- find the predicate nominative, if there is one.

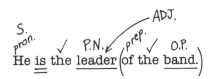

Additional Sentence to Analyze

The girl (by the door) will be the first singer (in the concert.)

(Diagrammed sentence: "The girl" — subject "girl"; "(by the door)" — prepositional phrase, ADJ., prep. "by", O.P. "door"; "will be" — verb; "the first singer" — adj. "first", P.N. "singer"; "(in the concert)" — prepositional phrase, ADJ., prep. "in", O.P. "concert")

Move on to Worksheet 27.

WORKSHEET

CARDS: All Parts of Speech Cards
        Noun Function Cards 1-5
NEW CONCEPTS: None

Worksheet 28 provides review of all concepts covered so far:
• Parts of Speech
• Prepositional Phrases
• Objects of Prepositions
• Words Modified by Adjectives and Adverbs
• Subjects
• Action and Linking Verbs
• Direct Objects
• Indirect Objects
• Predicate Nominatives

Move on to Worksheet 28.

Quiz

After completing Worksheet 28, students should be ready to take Quiz 4 using the clue cards if needed.

CARDS: All Parts of Speech Cards
                 Noun Function Cards 1-7
NEW CONCEPT: Nouns of Direct Address

Noun Function Card 6

6

**THE NOUN FUNCTIONS
COVERED UP TO THIS POINT ARE:**

Object of the preposition
Subject
Direct Object
Indirect Object
Predicate Nominative

Every sentence <u>must</u> have a subject.
The other noun functions may or
may not be present.

Have you identified a noun function for every
noun and every pronoun in the sentence?

YES? Go to next sentence.

NO? GO TO CARD #7 (PURPLE).

Noun Function Card 7

7

**IS THERE A NOUN SET OFF
BY COMMAS IN THE SENTENCE?**

NO? — Go back to card #1. You must have
made a mistake.

YES? — Does this noun name the person being
spoken to in the sentence?

EX: <u>Bob</u>, I <u>want</u> the ⟨milk.⟩

Is Bob being spoken to? YES.

Bob is a noun of direct address.
<u>Mark it N.D.A.</u>

Bob, I <u>want</u> the ⟨milk.⟩

If the noun set off by commas is not an
N.D.A. it is probably an <u>appositive</u>.

GO TO CARD #8 (LIGHT BLUE)

IMPORTANT INFORMATION FOR STUDENTS

- Nouns of direct address are nouns that name the person spoken to in the sentence.
- Nouns of direct address are set off with commas.

Example: Look at this, Stella.

- The abbreviation for a noun of direct address is *N.D.A.*

Sentence for Practice

Terry, you dropped a pencil.

Sentence Analyzed with Clue Cards

Sentence Analyzed with Symbols and Abbreviations

Use Noun Function Cards to:
• find the subject;
• determine whether the verb is action or linking;
• find the direct object, if there is one;
• find the indirect object, if there is one;
• find the predicate nominative, if there is one;
• find the noun of direct address, if there is one.

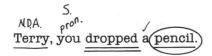

Move on to Worksheet 29.

CARDS: All Parts of Speech Cards
Noun Function Cards 1-8
NEW CONCEPT: Appositives

Noun Function Card 8

8   **FINDING AN APPOSITIVE**

An appositive is a noun set off by commas which
names the same person or thing named by a noun in
front of it.

           s.   ✔
EX: Mr. Jones, the teacher, is
prep. ✔   O.P.
(on the playground).

teacher is set off by commas.

teacher names the same person as the noun in
front of it (Mr. Jones).

teacher is an appositive. Mark it APP.

     s.   ✔   APP.
Mr. Jones, the teacher, is
prep. ✔   O.P.
(on the playground).

All nouns and pronouns must be labeled for their
noun function. If they are, go to the next sentence.
If they are not,

RETURN TO CARD #1 (RED)

┌─**IMPORTANT INFORMATION FOR STUDENTS**─┐

- An appositive is a noun that names the same person, place, thing, or idea as the noun preceding it.
- An appositive is usually set off with commas.

  Example: We will visit our state capital, Albany.

  Albany is set off with a comma. *Albany* is a noun that names the same thing as *capital*.

- The abbreviation for an appositive is *APP*.

Sentence for Practice

Gary, the new paperboy, sent us a bill today.

Sentence Analyzed with Clue Cards

 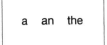  

Sentence Analyzed with Symbols and Abbreviations

Use Noun Function Cards to:
- find the subject;
- determine whether the verb is action or linking;
- find the direct object, if there is one;
- find the indirect object, if there is one;
- find the predicate nominative, if there is one;
- find the noun of direct address, if there is one;
- find the appositive, if there is one.

Remind the students that 1) all nouns and pronouns perform a noun function in a sentence and (2) no noun or pronoun can perform more than one noun function.

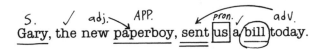

Move on to Worksheet 30.

Answer Keys
for Tests, Worksheets
and Quizzes

Pretest

Write your answers to the following questions on the lines at the right.

Sentence 1

The old truck chugged slowly along the highway.

1. Name the adjective.   *old*   1.
2. Name the adverb.   *slowly*   2.
3. Name the preposition.   *along*   3.
4. Name the subject.   *truck*   4.
5. Name the object of the preposition.   *highway*   5.
6. What word does *slowly* modify?   *chugged*   6.

Sentence 2

She gave Dan a nice gift yesterday.

7. Name the direct object.   *gift*   7.
8. Name the adverb.   *yesterday*   8.
9. Name the verb.   *gave*   9.
10. Name the pronoun.   *She*   10.
11. Name the article.   *a*   11.
12. Name the indirect object.   *Dan*   12.
13. What word does *nice* modify?   *gift*   13.

Sentence 3

Do not take a nap before dinner, Teddy.

14. How many nouns are there in Sentence 3? _____ *three* _____ 14.

15. Name the direct object. _____ *nap* _____ 15.

16. Name the noun of direct address. _____ *Teddy* _____ 16.

17. Name the subject. _____ *(you)* _____ 17.

18. Name the verb phrase. _____ *do take* _____ 18.

19. Name the adverb. _____ *not* _____ 19.

Sentence 4

They are ready for the game, and I hope they will win.

20. Name the coordinating conjunction. _____ *and* _____ 20.

21. Name the helping verb. _____ *will* _____ 21.

22. Name the "being" or "linking" verb. _____ *are* _____ 22.

23. How many subjects are there in Sentence 4? _____ *three* _____ 23.

24. Name the adjective. _____ *ready* _____ 24.

Sentence 5

Ouch, the stove is very hot!

25. Name the verb. _____ *is* _____ 25.

26. Name the adverb. _____ *very* _____ 26.

27. Name the interjection. _____ *Ouch* _____ 27.

28. Name the article. _____ *the* _____ 28.

Sentence 6

Donna and I are the new captains of the golf team.

29. How many adjectives are there in Sentence 6? _____ *two* _____ 29.

30. Name the object of the preposition. _____ *team* _____ 30.

31. Name the subject(s). _____ *Donna, I* _____ 31.

32. Name the predicate nominative. _____ *captains* _____ 32.

33. What part of speech is *golf*? _____ *adjective* _____ 33.

WORKSHEET

1

- Put a check (√) over the articles.
- Underline the nouns once.

1. The <u>button</u> on the <u>doorbell</u> rings in the <u>house</u>.

2. We opened an old <u>chest</u> in the <u>attic</u>.

3. She took a <u>plane</u> to the <u>college</u>.

4. The <u>man</u> took the <u>kitten</u> into the <u>house</u>.

5. A <u>girl</u> in the <u>class</u> quickly found the <u>hamster</u>.

6. The <u>doctor</u> left an <u>umbrella</u> on the <u>table</u>.

7. He called a <u>plumber</u>; the <u>drainpipe</u> was very clogged.

8. Yesterday the best <u>team</u> won the big <u>game</u>.

9. The variety <u>show</u> was very good.

10. The <u>monster</u> in the <u>movie</u> frightened me.

11. The <u>farmer</u> raises <u>cows</u> and <u>horses</u>.

12. The <u>team</u> was happy with the new <u>coach</u>.

WORKSHEET

- Put a check (√) over articles.
- Underline all common and proper nouns once.
- Remember that proper nouns made of more than one word are underlined with one continous line.

1. Jacob moved from Detroit to San Diego.

2. Nettie DeSisto was a fan of Elvis Presley.

3. Ms. Brady is a good citizen.

4. We have an idea for the game.

5. I saw Ms. Frye at the grocery store today.

6. Bernard Roth and Sally Mason went to the opera.

7. We saw seals and whales at Marineland in Florida.

8. Carol Frost is a ✓ pilot for Trans World Airlines.

9. The ✓ United States is close to Canada on the ✓ map.

10. The ✓ Dallas Cowboys won the ✓ Super Bowl.

11. The real ✓ name for the ✓ dog is Clyde.

12. They watched *Gone with the Wind* on television.

1. The   <u>governor</u>   signed   the   <u>bill</u>   after   the   <u>debate.</u>

2. He   raises   <u>roses</u>   and   <u>tulips</u>   in   the   <u>backyard.</u>

3. During   the   <u>summer,</u>   <u>Wesley</u>   and   <u>Megan</u>   go

   to   an   overnight   <u>camp.</u>

4. <u>Bob Hope</u>   gave   a   <u>show</u>   for   the   <u>soldiers</u>

   in   <u>Saudi Arabia</u>.

5. Be   careful;   we   have   seen   <u>bears</u>   in   the   <u>park.</u>

6. We saw no <u>troopers</u> ✓ on the <u>road</u> near the <u>accident</u>. ✓

7. She went to medical <u>school</u> at <u>Harvard University</u>.

8. <u>Colorado</u> and <u>Wyoming</u> are west of <u>St. Louis.</u>

9. The <u>tools</u> ✓ in the <u>shed</u> ✓ were returned to <u>Mr. Nasser.</u>

10. They attended a <u>party</u> ✓ on <u>New Year's Eve.</u>

11. <u>Don Martin</u> arrived on a ✓ crowded <u>bus.</u>

12. <u>Uncle Karl</u> took me to a <u>game</u> ✓ at <u>Bass River Park.</u>

WORKSHEET

- Put a check (√) over articles.
- Underline nouns once.
- Write *pron.* over personal pronouns.

1. Shall *pron.* I tell *pron.* them about √ the <u>party</u>?

2. <u>Florida</u> is pleasant during √ the <u>winter</u>, <u>Leo</u>.

3. √ A brave <u>hiker</u> climbed <u>Mt. Washington</u>.

4. On <u>February 5th</u>, *pron.* they will meet *pron.* us in <u>Chicago</u>.

5. *pron.* He and √ the <u>boss</u> make important <u>decisions</u> together.

6. <u>World War II</u> was over by <u>1946.</u>

7. *pron.* You will see *pron.* her in <u>school</u> tomorrow.

8. <u>Worms</u> ✓ in the <u>garden</u> make the <u>soil</u> ✓ healthy.

9. They *pron.* went to <u>St. Luke's Hospital</u> during visiting <u>hours.</u>

10. She *pron.* would enjoy an <u>afternoon</u> ✓ at a <u>museum.</u> ✓

11. On <u>Independence Day,</u> we *pron.* celebrate the <u>birth</u> ✓

of the <u>country.</u> ✓

WORKSHEET

- Put a check (√) over articles.
- Underline nouns once.
- Write *pron.* over personal pronouns.

1. The √ knights returned from the royal √ tournament.

2. During the day, √ owls and bats sleep in the √ trees.

3. *pron.* She and *pron.* I slowly climbed the √ hill on bicycles.

4. The championship game was played on a √ muddy field. √

5. *pron.* He and *pron.* I are officers in the √ Lions Club.

6. Ms. Batal, a √ lawyer, came to the √ house today.

7. Johnny, will *pron.* you please pass *pron.* us the √ cake?

8. Early in the twentieth <u>century</u>, <u>people</u> did not

have <u>radios</u>.

9. They will go to the <u>game</u> tomorrow with <u>Aunt Louise</u>.

10. <u>San Francisco</u> is on the <u>coast</u> of the <u>Pacific Ocean</u>.

11. The <u>election</u> is not over, but we know the <u>results</u>.

12. <u>Marcia</u> presented an <u>award</u> to him at the <u>banquet</u>.

• In each blank, fill in the correct form of the verb.

1. I will _____ *kick* _____   4. I will _____ *eat* _____

   Yesterday I _____ *kicked* _____   Yesterday I _____ *ate* _____

   I have _____ *kicked* _____   I have _____ *eaten* _____

2. I will _____ *see* _____   5. I will _____ *write* _____

   Yesterday I _____ *saw* _____   Yesterday I _____ *wrote* _____

   I have _____ *seen* _____   I have _____ *written* _____

3. I will _____ *speak* _____   6. I will _____ *open* _____

   Yesterday I _____ *spoke* _____   Yesterday I _____ *opened* _____

   I have _____ *spoken* _____   I have _____ *opened* _____

• Put a check (√) over articles.
• Underline nouns once.
• Write *pron.* over personal pronouns.
• Underline verbs twice.

1. We ate fruit and nuts after dinner.

2. The new mayor was a speaker at the parade.

3. The <u>engineer</u> ✓ <u>jumped</u> from the <u>train</u> ✓ carefully.

4. <u>Mr. Sonbolian</u> <u>greeted</u> her. *proh.* at the <u>door</u> ✓.

5. She <u>swims</u> *proh.* twenty <u>laps</u> in the <u>pool</u> ✓ before <u>breakfast</u>.

WORKSHEET

- Put a check (√) over articles.
- Underline nouns once.
- Write *pron.* over personal pronouns.
- Underline verbs twice.

1. Florence Nightingale helped many soldiers

   in the √ Crimean War.

2. *pron.* I √ wanted a good performance yesterday.

3. The √ young teacher collects stamps and coins.

4. A √ tall gentleman stood in the √ doorway.

5. *pron.* We worked hard in class today.

6. Flash caught a √ mouse in the √ cellar.

7. Before a <u>storm</u>, the <u>air</u> <u>is</u> heavy and still.

8. <u>Seth</u> <u>Dator</u> <u>writes</u> <u>poems</u>, and I <u>write</u> stories. *pron.*

9. Early in the twentieth <u>century</u>, <u>children</u> <u>worked</u>

   in <u>factories</u>.

10. A <u>firefighter</u> <u>helped</u> the <u>child</u> down the <u>ladder</u>.

11. The tired <u>swimmers</u> <u>rested</u> on the <u>beach</u>.

12. <u>Olivia</u> <u>held</u> the <u>stopwatch</u> during the <u>race</u>.

QUIZ

(to be taken after completing Worksheet 7)

- Put a check (√) over articles.
- Underline all common and proper nouns once.
- Write *pron.* over personal pronouns.
- Underline verbs twice.

1. An honest person deserves respect from us.

2. He and I enjoyed a fancy meal.

3. In some countries, the government controls

    what people read.

4. *Little Women* is a favorite book of many children.

5. Henry Williams and Peter Hawkins fought for the Union

    in the Civil War.

6. A pot of soup simmered on the stove.

7. We _found_ an unusual _seashell_ ✓ at the _beach._
   pron.

8. _Helen Keller_ _was_ blind and deaf, but she *pron.*

   overcame these _handicaps._

9. _South Junior High_ and _Parker_ _are_ ✓ the

   new _schools_ in _town._

10. On _July 4th,_ they always _go_ ✓ to the _country_
    pron.

    for a _picnic._ ✓

Bonus

   In _1964,_ _Martin Luther King, Jr._ _received_ ✓ the

   Nobel Prize for _peace._

WORKSHEET

- Put a check (√) over articles.
- Underline nouns once.
- Write *pron.* over personal pronouns.
- Underline verbs twice.
- Watch for helping verbs.

1. I have gone to the movies already today.

2. The White Sox might be in the playoffs now.

3. You will find the papers on the desk.

4. All students should be polite in class.

5. The giraffes had eaten the leaves from the tops

of the trees.

6. The heavy rains kept the farmers from the fields.

7. I *pron.* <u>may</u> <u>try</u>✓ some of the new <u>games</u> tomorrow.

8. A <u>student</u>✓ <u>can</u> <u>write</u> a <u>report</u>✓ in the <u>library</u>✓.

9. The <u>company</u> <u>might</u>✓ <u>move</u> to <u>New</u> <u>York</u>.

10. I *pron.* <u>do</u> not <u>enjoy</u> horror <u>movies</u>.

11. The <u>baby</u>✓ <u>could</u> <u>speak</u> very clearly.

12. The <u>mittens</u>✓ <u>were</u> <u>knitted</u> by <u>Grandmother</u>.

WORKSHEET

- Put a check (√) over articles.
- Underline nouns once.
- Write *pron.* over personal pronouns.
- Underline verbs twice.
- Watch for contractions.

1. *pron.* She's not afraid of snakes or mice.

2. *pron.* We'll miss *pron.* them over the ✓ the weekend.

3. *pron.* I'll stay here during ✓ the parade.

4. *pron.* We've counted ✓ the pennies in ✓ the jar.

5. *pron.* He'll read ✓ the first story in ✓ the book.

6. *pron.* They'd like ✓ the pizza better with peppers on *pron.* it.

7. *pron.* You're ✓ the best dog in ✓ the show, Sam.

8. I've *pron.* never <u>been</u> to <u>Japan</u> or <u>China</u>.

9. We'd *pron.* <u>enjoy</u> a <u>trip</u> ✓ to <u>South</u> <u>America</u>.

10. I'm *pron.* sure it's *pron.* correct.

11. They're *pron.* in <u>college</u>, but I'm *pron.* not.

12. You'll *pron.* <u>hide</u> behind the <u>tree</u> ✓.

WORKSHEET

• Identify all parts of speech that have been learned so far.
• Watch for interrogative sentences.

1. Is Detroit located near the Great Lakes?

2. They'll be late for the party, and I'll be angry.

3. Robin Hood stole from rich people and helped

   poor people.

4. Can you be in Denver on January 8, 1994?

5. I thought you'd give her a chance.

6. Do the peanuts make you thirsty?

7. The little children enjoyed the clowns at the circus.

8. Did Tanya go into the store for a newspaper?

9. The boy smiled at the new puppy.

10. She's *pron.* been in Africa with the Peace Corps.

11. The president lives in the White House

    in Washington, D.C.

12. Will the old riverboat ever carry passengers again?

WORKSHEET

- Identify all parts of speech learned so far.
- Remember to write *adj.* over adjectives.

1. The young pony is cute and frisky.

2. We'll have hot rolls and eggs today.

3. The deep cut on the arm has healed.

4. On winter mornings, the old car always starts.

5. Ramona spilled green paint on the kitchen floor.

6. A thin layer of dust covered the floor.

7. The sharp drill will go through the wood.

8. He <u>loved</u> the beautiful <u>beaches</u> in <u>Puerto Rico</u>.

pron.   ✓   *adj.*

9. Stormy <u>weather</u> <u>sells</u> umbrellas at the department <u>store</u>.

adj.   ✓   *adj.*

10. The <u>meal</u> <u>was</u> delicious at the <u>Log Cabin Inn</u>.

✓   *adj.*   ✓

11. The cold <u>water</u> <u>refreshed</u> the thirsty <u>bikers</u>.

✓   *adj.*   ✓   *adj.*

12. <u>I'll</u> <u>look</u> for the red <u>bottle</u> on the back <u>shelf</u>.

pron.   ✓   *adj.*   ✓   *adj.*

WORKSHEET

- Identify all parts of speech learned so far.
- Remember to write *adj.* over adjectives and *adv.* over adverbs.

1. The <u>bullfrog</u> quickly <u>hopped</u> across the muddy <u>bank</u>.
   (adv. over quickly; adj. over muddy)

2. The <u>fields</u> <u>are</u> pretty in the French <u>painting</u>.
   (adj. over pretty; adj. over French)

3. Today we <u>had</u> a <u>picnic</u> under the elm <u>tree</u>.
   (adv. over Today; pron. over we; adj. over elm)

4. <u>We're</u> happy about the new <u>puppy</u>.
   (pron. over We; adj. over happy; adj. over new)

5. <u>Business</u> <u>will</u> slowly <u>improve</u> later in the <u>year</u>.
   (adv. over slowly; adv. over later)

6. <u>Will</u> you <u>stay</u> and <u>have</u> a <u>snack</u> with us?
   (pron. over you; pron. over us)

7. <u>We've</u> <u>been</u> on the <u>trail</u> for three <u>days</u>.
   (pron. over We; adj. over three)

8. The rubber band [✓] wrapped [adj.] the papers [✓] tightly. [adv.]

9. South America isn't [adv.] cold [adj.] near the Equator. [✓]

10. I [pron.] recently [adv.] read To Kill a Mockingbird.

11. The pencil [✓] is [adj.] dull; I'll [pron.] sharpen it. [pron.]

12. Never [adv.] dive into shallow water, [adj.] Betsy.

13. An old [✓] necklace [adj.] was found here [adv.] yesterday. [adv.]

WORKSHEET 13

• Identify all parts of speech learned so far.

1. The carpenter carefully **cut** the **lumber** for the **cabinets**.
   [checkmark over carpenter] adv. (over cut) [checkmark over lumber] [checkmark over cabinets]

2. **I'll** always **buy** groceries on the **weekends**.
   pron. (over I'll) adv. (over always) [checkmark over weekends]

3. A shiny red **apple** **appeared** on the **desk** today.
   [checkmark over A] adj. (over shiny) adj. (over red) [checkmark over desk] adv. (over today)

4. **Elephants** **aren't** often **found** in European **zoos**.
   adv. (over aren't) adv. (over often) adj. (over European) zoos

5. First, you **connect** the **wires** to the small **battery**.
   adv. (over First) pron. (over you) [checkmark over the] [checkmark over the] adj. (over small)

6. The **students** **were** good **listeners**, and **they** **asked**
   [checkmark over students] adj. (over good) pron. (over they)

   a few **questions**.
   [checkmark over a] adj. (over few)

7. You *pron.* <u>returned</u> ✓ from the hardware *adj.* <u>store</u> *adv.* quickly.

8. We *pron.* <u>should</u> <u>divide</u> ✓ the <u>cards</u> into equal *adj.* <u>piles.</u>

9. *adv.* Tomorrow she'<u>ll</u> *pron.* <u>take</u> a ✓ <u>bus</u> to <u>Miami</u> <u>Beach.</u>

10. <u>Can</u> *pron.* you <u>see</u> *pron.* it *adv.* now, <u>Ms.</u> <u>Johnson?</u>

11. <u>Marcus</u> <u>couldn't</u> *adv.* <u>decide</u> on ✓ a <u>name</u> for the ✓ <u>kitten.</u>

12. <u>Henri</u> <u>put</u> ✓ the <u>hammer</u> and <u>nails</u> *adv.* neatly

on the <u>workbench.</u> ✓

13. You *pron.* <u>might</u> <u>leave</u> ✓ the <u>dog</u> *adv.* outside.

QUIZ

(to be taken after completing Worksheet 13)

- Put a check (√) over articles.
- Underline nouns once.
- Write *pron.* over personal pronouns.
- Underline verbs twice.
- Write *adj.* over adjectives.
- Write *adv.* over adverbs.

1. I'm not in the chess club, Ms. Bergeron.

2. In the general store, you can buy candy

   for a penny.

3. It often snows heavily during the winter months

   in the Midwest.

4. Isn't Butch a builder in New Orleans?

5. She had taped the important message securely

   on the refrigerator door.

6. Tomorrow *adv.* they'll *pron.* learn ✓ the correct *adj.* bus *adj.* route.

7. Could *pron.* we have ✓ the surprise *adj.* party here? *adv.*

8. She *pron.* drew a large ✓ *adj.* circle around it *pron.* with chalk.

9. Immediately *adv.* we *pron.* became *adj.* suspicious.

10. He *pron.* might be happy *adj.* now. *adv.*

Bonus

Won't *adv.* you *pron.* ever *adv.* go outside? *adv.*

WORKSHEET

- Identify all parts of speech learned so far.
- Draw arrows from adjectives and adverbs to the words they modify.

1. Pure <u>water</u> <u>is</u> delicious on a hot <u>day</u>. *adj.* *adj.* *adj.*

2. <u>Baseball</u> <u>wasn't</u> always popular in <u>Japan</u>. *adv.* *adv.* *adj.*

3. The bright <u>torch</u> <u>lit</u> the <u>cave</u> very nicely. *adj.* *adv.* *adv.*

4. <u>Aunt Dolores</u> <u>phoned</u> and <u>told</u> us about the <u>blizzard</u> *pron.*

   in <u>New England</u>.

5. Tiny <u>snakes</u> <u>are</u> sometimes quite dangerous. *adj.* *adv.* *adv.* *adj.*

6. We <u>will</u> <u>plant</u> an oak <u>tree</u> there. *pron.* *adj.* *adv.*

7. The spaceship landed safely on the back side

of the moon.

8. I won't go too far into the dense jungle.

9. Always close the windows during a thunderstorm.

10. The ugly fish suddenly frightened the brave diver.

11. The plumber can't fix the leaky sink today.

12. Luckily, I found the coins on the rug.

WORKSHEET 15

- Identify all parts of speech learned so far.
- Draw arrows from adjectives and adverbs to the words they modify.
- Remember to write *prep.* over a preposition and put a (in front of a preposition.

1. We hid the presents (under the bed.

2. They played outside (near the pond yesterday.

3. Aren't you hungry (in the morning?

4. They dug (for clams (on the sandbar (at low tide.

5. You may go (into the house (for a drink.

6. (In Australia, it's winter (in August.

7. Celia often rides (to school (with Ms. Pope.

8. You shouldn't talk too loudly (during the movie.

9. She'll be (at the race (on Saturday.

10. I was sick (on the day (of the festival.

11. She laughed (at the silly joke (in the paper.

12. Roberto will take a bus (to Mexico City today.

- Identify all parts of speech learned so far.
- Draw arrows from adjectives and adverbs to the words they modify.
- Write *O.P.* over the object of a preposition.
- Enclose prepositional phrases within parentheses.
- Label each prepositional phrase with either *ADJ.* or *ADV.*
- Draw arrows from prepositional phrases to the words they modify.

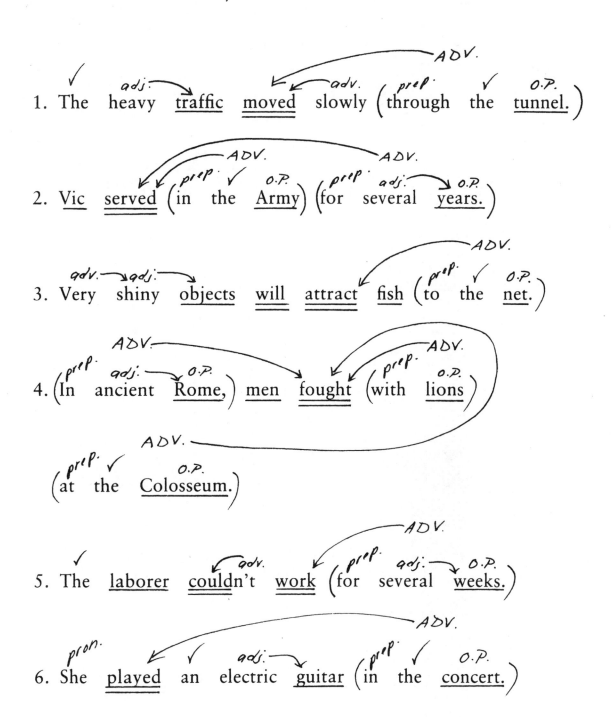

1. The heavy traffic moved slowly (through the tunnel.)

2. Vic served (in the Army) (for several years.)

3. Very shiny objects will attract fish (to the net.)

4. (In ancient Rome,) men fought (with lions) (at the Colosseum.)

5. The laborer couldn't work (for several weeks.)

6. She played an electric guitar (in the concert.)

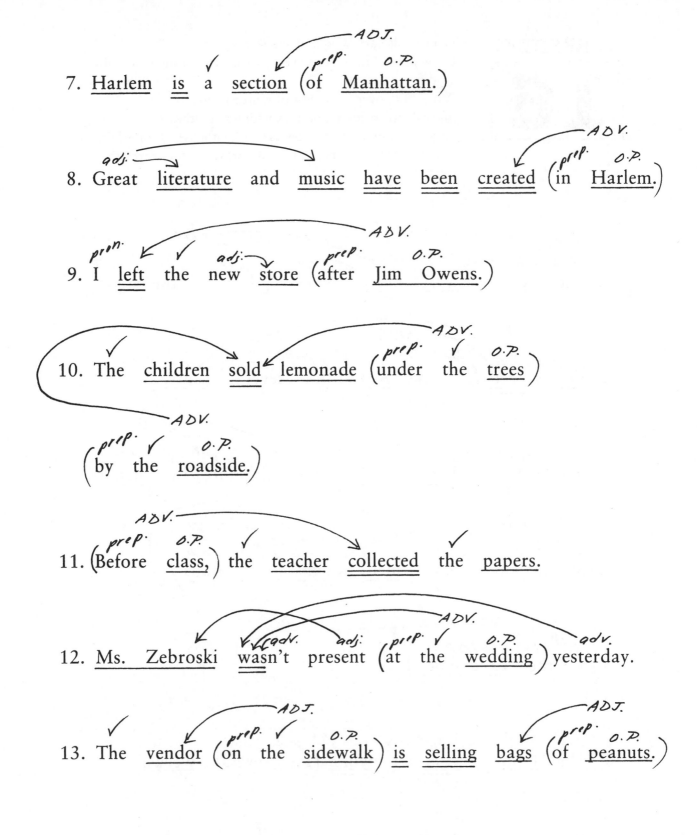

7. Harlem <u>is</u> a section (of Manhattan.)

8. Great literature and music have been created (in Harlem.)

9. I <u>left</u> the new store (after Jim Owens.)

10. The children <u>sold</u> lemonade (under the trees) (by the roadside.)

11. (Before class,) the teacher collected the papers.

12. <u>Ms. Zebroski</u> <u>wasn't</u> present (at the wedding) yesterday.

13. The vendor (on the sidewalk) <u>is</u> selling bags (of peanuts.)

WORKSHEET

- Identify all parts of speech learned so far.
- Draw arrows from adjectives and adverbs to the words they modify.
- Write *O.P.* over the object of a preposition.
- Enclose prepositional phrases within parentheses.
- Label each prepositional phrase with either *ADJ.* or *ADV.*
- Draw arrows from prepositional phrases to the words they modify.

1. (Beyond the hill,) we found a beautiful little pond.

2. Fido quickly ran and hid (under the porch.)

3. I don't like milk (in coffee.)

4. She knows the guest (from Lebanon.)

5. She bought a new car (at the local dealership.)

6. We have big problems (with the new highway.)

7. A long letter (from Mr. Chung) arrived today.

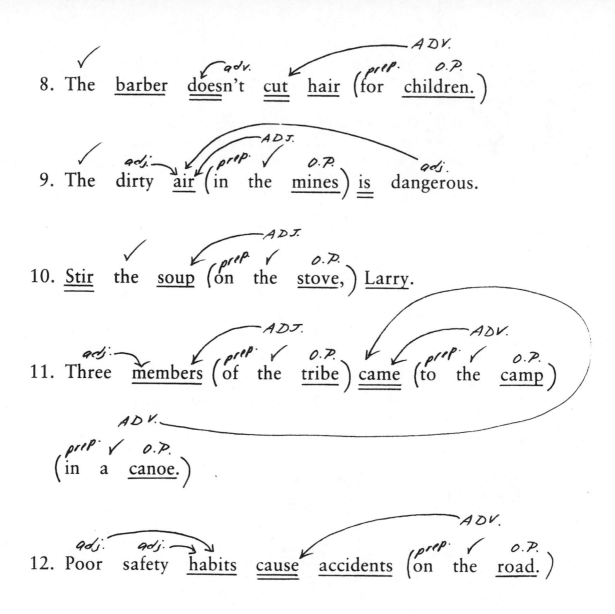

8. The <u>barber</u> <u>doesn't</u> <u>cut</u> hair (for <u>children.</u>)

9. The dirty <u>air</u> (in the <u>mines</u>) <u>is</u> dangerous.

10. <u>Stir</u> the <u>soup</u> (on the <u>stove,</u>) Larry.

11. Three <u>members</u> (of the <u>tribe</u>) <u>came</u> (to the <u>camp</u>) (in a <u>canoe.</u>)

12. Poor safety <u>habits</u> <u>cause</u> accidents (on the <u>road.</u>)

WORKSHEET 18

- Identify all parts of speech learned so far.
- Remember to write *c.c.* over coordinating conjunctions.
- Draw arrows from adjectives and adverbs to the words they modify.
- Write *O.P.* over the object of a preposition.
- Enclose prepositional phrases within parentheses.
- Label each prepositional phrase with either *ADJ.* or *ADV.*
- Draw arrows from prepositional phrases to the words they modify.

1. She's very confident, but he's nervous.

2. It was cold and windy (on the shore) (of Lake Huron.)

3. The machine (in the shop) was old yet useful.

4. The mysterious woman left, but she'll return soon.

5. The library is (down the street) and (around the corner.)

6. Armando is very happy, for he will go (to Acapulco) tomorrow.

7. I <u>will</u> <u>invite</u> Anna or Rosalie (to the <u>race</u>)
    pron.   c.c.   prep. ✓   O.P. ADV.

(at the <u>club.</u>)
prep. ✓ O.P.   ADJ.

8. The <u>Marine Corps</u> and the <u>Navy</u> <u>have</u> new <u>uniforms.</u>
        ✓   c.c.   ✓   adj.

9. <u>Were</u> you (at <u>home</u>) or (in <u>school</u>) yesterday?
    pron.   prep. O.P. ADV. c.c. prep. O.P. ADV.   adv.

10. The <u>pencils</u> and <u>pens</u> <u>haven't</u> <u>arrived</u> yet.
      ✓   c.c.   adv.   adv.

11. <u>We'll</u> <u>visit</u> the <u>museums</u> and art <u>galleries</u>
    pron.   ✓   c.c.   adj.

(in <u>Los Angeles.</u>)
prep. O.P.   ADV.

12. They <u>must</u> <u>improve,</u> or <u>they'll</u> never <u>win.</u>
    pron.   c.c. pron.   adv.

WORKSHEET

- Identify all parts of speech learned so far.
- Draw arrows from adjectives and adverbs to the words they modify.
- Write *O.P.* over the object of a preposition.
- Enclose prepositional phrases within parentheses.
- Label each prepositional phrase with either *ADJ.* or *ADV.*
- Draw arrows from prepositional phrases to the words they modify.

1. I want a new car, but I can't afford it.

2. Will you go (with us) or stay (with her?)

3. The operation was a success; he'll be healthy soon.

4. The rabbit ran (across the field) and (into the woods.)

5. Fumiko bought bread, jam, and cookies (for lunch.)

6. (In a few minutes,) you'll learn the answer.

7. Maria studied hard, and she passed the test.

8. She found three books, but she couldn't choose (among them.)

9. The lion cubs lay (in the sun) (near the edge) (of the river.)

10. The steel workers asked the boss a question.

11. Recently, many people (from Cambodia) have arrived (in the United States.)

12. We made too much noise and frightened the birds away.

WORKSHEET 20

- Identify all parts of speech learned so far.
- Remember to write ! over interjections.
- Draw arrows from adjectives and adverbs to the words they modify.
- Write O.P. over the object of a preposition.
- Enclose prepositional phrases within parentheses.
- Label each prepositional phrase with either *ADJ.* or *ADV.*
- Draw arrows from prepositional phrases to the words they modify.

1. Hey, didn't you see me?

2. We would have gone, but we were busy.

3. Help me, Tina; I need some information.

4. Yuck! I hate stale cookies.

5. The teenagers loved the loud music (on the radio.)

6. The old car made funny noises.

7. Ah, now I understand the problem!

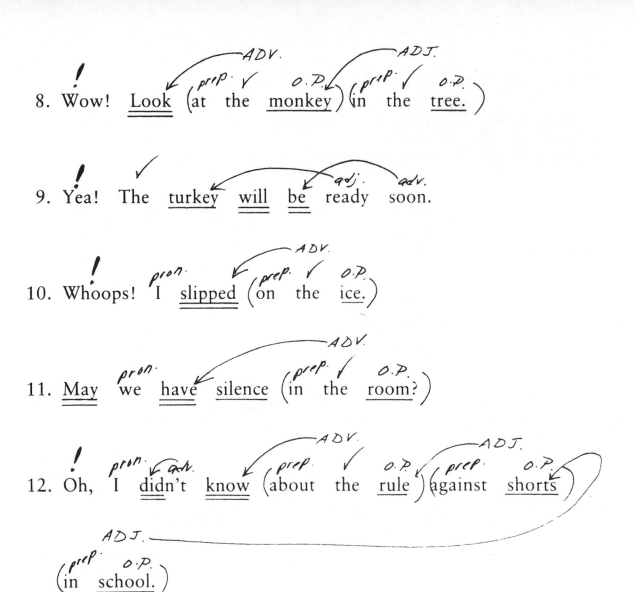

8. Wow! <u>Look</u> (at the <u>monkey</u>) (in the <u>tree.</u>)

9. Yea! The <u>turkey</u> <u>will</u> <u>be</u> ready soon.

10. Whoops! I <u>slipped</u> (on the <u>ice.</u>)

11. <u>May</u> we <u>have</u> silence (in the <u>room?</u>)

12. Oh, I <u>didn't</u> <u>know</u> (about the <u>rule</u>) (against <u>shorts</u>) (in <u>school.</u>)

- Identify all parts of speech learned so far.
- Draw arrows from adjectives and adverbs to the words they modify.
- Write *O.P.* over the object of a preposition.
- Enclose prepositional phrases within parentheses.
- Label each prepositional phrase with either *ADJ.* or *ADV.*
- Draw arrows from prepositional phrases to the words they modify.

1. It *is* much colder (in Moscow) today.

2. The coach gave the football team a fiery pep talk (before the game.)

3. Frost damaged the vegetables (in the garden.)

4. Oh, I didn't know the answer.

5. I'll read the long report (to her.)

6. She could see a doctor (about the injury.)

7. Read the directions and start the motor.
   (marks: ✓ over Read, ✓ over directions, c.c. over and, ✓ over start, ✓ over motor)

8. The happy boy lighted the candles (on the cake.)
   (✓ over The, adj. over happy pointing to boy, ✓ over lighted, ✓ over candles, prep. over on, ✓ over the, o.p. over cake, ADJ. arrow)

9. A policewoman gave Carmen a ticket yesterday (in Mayberry.)
   (✓ over A, gave, adv. over yesterday, ADV. arrow, prep. over in, o.p. over Mayberry)

10. The small child tossed the ball (into the air.)
    (✓ over The, adj. over small pointing to child, ✓ over ball, ADV. arrow, prep. over into, ✓ over the, o.p. over air)

11. (After one lesson,) Vito could ski beautifully.
    (prep. over After, adj. over one, o.p. over lesson, ADV. arrow, could, ski, adv. over beautifully)

12. You can connect the dots (on the paper.)
    (pron. over You, can, connect, ✓ over the, dots, ADJ. arrow, prep. over on, ✓ over the, o.p. over paper)

(to be taken after completing Worksheet 21)

- Identify all parts of speech learned so far.
- Draw arrows from adjectives and adverbs to the words they modify.
- Write *O.P.* over the object of a preposition.
- Enclose prepositional phrases within parentheses.
- Label each prepositional phrase with either *ADJ.* or *ADV.*
- Draw arrows from prepositional phrases to the words they modify.

1. Amy and Erin won't be (at home) today.

2. I have never been (to Wyoming,) but I am

    going there soon.

3. Oh, the summer is passing too quickly!

4. A wise person eats the right food and

    gets enough exercise.

5. (During the storm,) we stood (in the doorway)

    (of the building.)

6. Good strawberries aren't always available.

adj. *adv.* *adv.* *adj.*

7. (At the end) (of the pep rally,) the new cheerleader was very hoarse.

ADV. *prep.* *o.p.* *prep.* *adj.* *o.p.* *ADJ.* *adj.* *adv.* *adj.*

8. Do you know the rules (of the game) or shall I tell them (to you?)

pron. *prep.* *o.p.* *ADJ.* *c.c.* *pron.* *pron.* *ADV.* *o.p.* *prep.* *pron.*

9. (At the Olympics,) Olga Korbut did a backwards somersault (on the parallel bars.)

prep. *o.p.* *ADV.* *adj.* *prep.* *adj.* *o.p.* *ADV.*

10. Close the back door (before dinner,) Marcello.

adj. *prep.* *o.p.* *ADV.*

Bonus

Wow I'm already rather old (for the team.)

pron. *adv.* *adv.* *adj.* *prep.* *o.p.* *ADV.*

WORKSHEET

- Identify all parts of speech learned so far.
- Don't forget that some pronouns may be omitted. When this is the case, write in the pronoun and enclose it within parentheses.
- Draw arrows from adjectives and adverbs to the words they modify.
- Write *O.P.* over the object of a preposition.
- Enclose prepositional phrases within parentheses.
- Label each prepositional phrase with either *ADJ.* or *ADV.*
- Draw arrows from prepositional phrases to the words they modify.

1. (You) Empty the garbage now.

2. (You) Hurry home (after the game,) Felicia.

3. (I) Thank you again (for the ride) (to the dance.)

4. Do you need the tools and the ladder?

5. Hey! (You) Leave the pool immediately.

6. (On January 1st,) we will go (to the Cotton Bowl.)

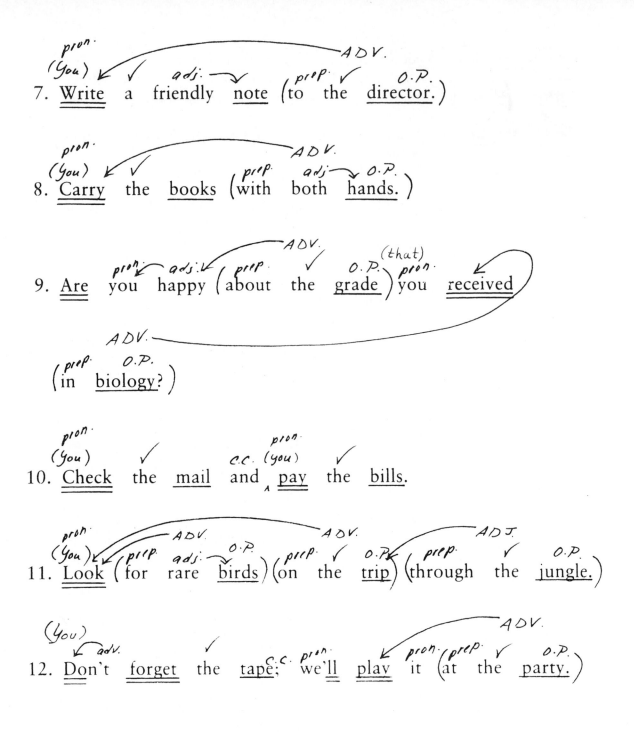

7. Write a friendly note (to the director.)

8. Carry the books (with both hands.)

9. Are you happy (about the grade) you received
(in biology?)

10. Check the mail and pay the bills.

11. Look (for rare birds)(on the trip)(through the jungle.)

12. Don't forget the tape; we'll play it (at the party.)

- Identify all parts of speech learned so far.
- Draw arrows from adjectives and adverbs to the words they modify.
- Write *O.P.* over the object of a preposition.
- Enclose prepositional phrases within parentheses.
- Label each prepositional phrase with either *ADJ.* or *ADV.*
- Draw arrows from prepositional phrases to the words they modify.
- Use Noun Function Card 1; put an *S.* over each subject.

1. Mother rides a bus (to the office.)

2. We had a flat tire (on the busy highway.)

3. Is he (in the office) today, Ms. Najinsky?

4. Mr. Goldberg took the baseball team (to Yankee Stadium)
(for the game)(with the Detroit Tigers.)

5. The door won't open; I can't get outside.

6. The big, shaggy collie produced ten pups.

7. George Washington Carver found many uses (for peanut shells.)

8. Grandmother volunteers (at the new community hospital.)

9. Riverboat rides don't make me ill.

10. (After the boat trip,) we will walk (to the center) (of town.)

11. Dr. Wu is an excellent dentist.

12. She and I won't arrive (until Sunday.)

- Identify all parts of speech learned so far.
- Draw arrows from adjectives and adverbs to the words they modify.
- Write *O.P.* over the object of a preposition.
- Enclose prepositional phrases within parentheses.
- Label each prepositional phrase with either *ADJ.* or *ADV.*
- Draw arrows from prepositional phrases to the words they modify.
- Use Noun Function Card 1; put an *S.* over each subject.
- Use Noun Function Card 2; tell whether the main verb is action or linking by circling the correct letter at the end of each sentence.

1. The rodeo clown jumped (into the barrel.) (A) L

2. She is (on the class list.) A (L)

3. (On Saturdays,) we eat dinner (at different restaurants.) (A) L

4. You seem sad today. A (L)

5. The ugly duckling became a swan. A (L)

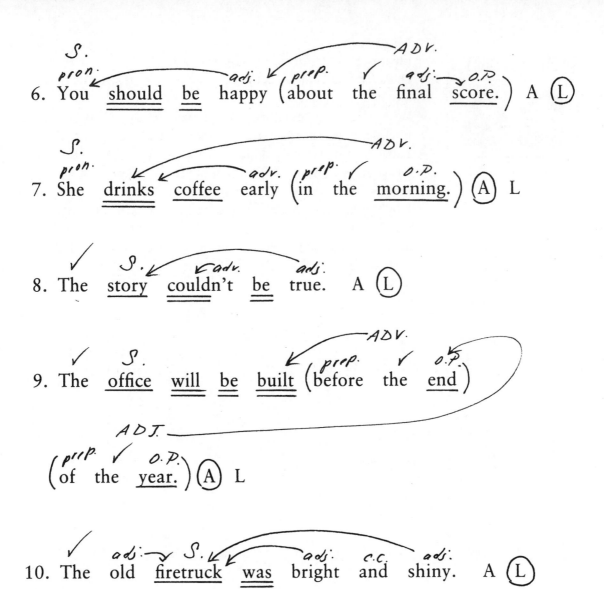

6. You should be happy (about the final score.) A (L)

7. She drinks coffee early (in the morning.) (A) L

8. The story couldn't be true. A (L)

9. The office will be built (before the end) (of the year.) (A) L

10. The old firetruck was bright and shiny. A (L)

- Identify all parts of speech learned so far.
- If a pronoun has been omitted, write it in and enclose it within parentheses.
- Draw arrows from adjectives and adverbs to the words they modify.
- Write *O.P.* over the object of a preposition.
- Enclose prepositional phrases within parentheses.
- Label each prepositional phrase with either *ADJ.* or *ADV.*
- Draw arrows from prepositional phrases to the words they modify.
- Use Noun Function Cards 1–3:
    Put an *S.* over each subject.
    Circle each direct object.

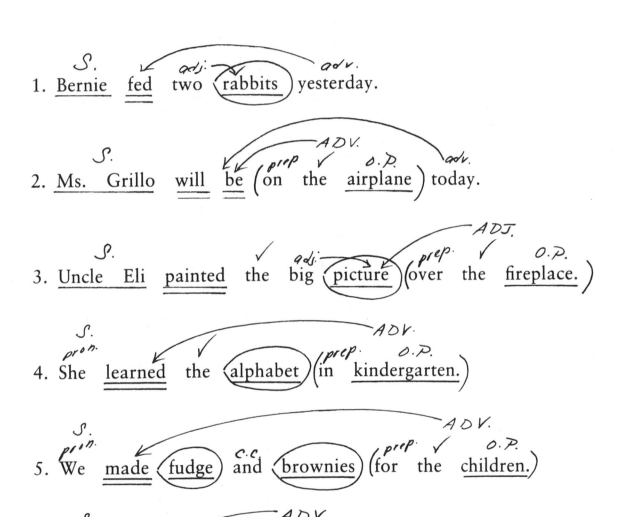

1. Bernie fed two rabbits yesterday.

2. Ms. Grillo will be (on the airplane) today.

3. Uncle Eli painted the big picture (over the fireplace.)

4. She learned the alphabet (in kindergarten.)

5. We made fudge and brownies (for the children.)

6. She walked (down the cellar stairs.)

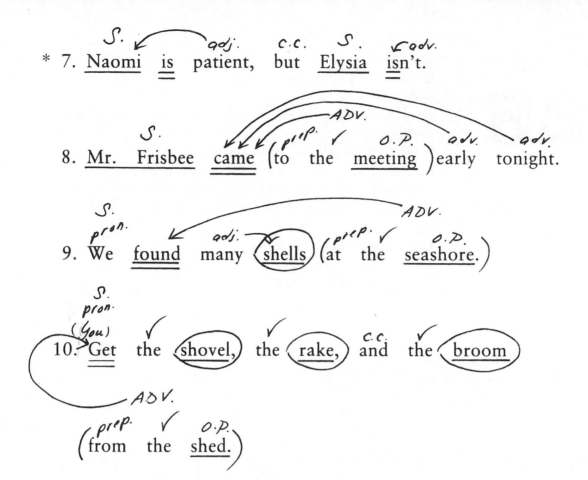

* 7. Naomi is patient, but Elysia isn't.

8. Mr. Frisbee came (to the meeting) early tonight.

9. We found many (shells) (at the seashore.)

10. Get the (shovel,) the (rake,) and the (broom (from the shed.)

* Optional: A student may put *(patient)* as an ellipsis; it is an adjective
modifying Elysia.

- Identify all parts of speech learned so far.
- Draw arrows from adjectives and adverbs to the words they modify.
- Write *O.P.* over the object of a preposition.
- Enclose prepositional phrases within parentheses.
- Label each prepositional phrase with either *ADJ.* or *ADV.*
- Draw arrows from prepositional phrases to the words they modify.
- Use Noun Function Cards 1–4:
    Put an *S.* over each subject.
    Circle each direct object.
    Put a box around each indirect object.

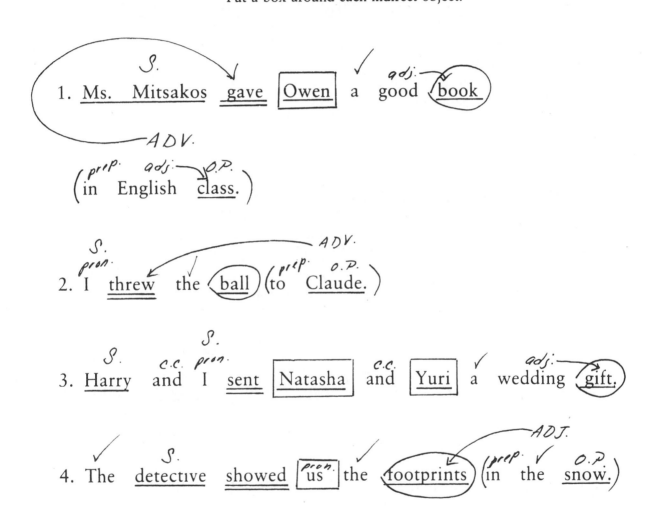

1. Ms. Mitsakos gave Owen a good book (in English class.)

2. I threw the ball (to Claude.)

3. Harry and I sent Natasha and Yuri a wedding gift.

4. The detective showed us the footprints (in the snow.)

5. The accent taught the reckless [driver] an important
lesson.

6. The committee gave [Michael Jordan] an (award)
(after the season.)

7. We picked a (map) (for the trip.)

8. The message (from the ship) was urgent.

9. Mother filled the (jar) (with pennies, nickels, and dimes.)

10. The cook added extra (vegetables) (to the soup.)

WORKSHEET

- Identify all parts of speech learned so far.
- Draw arrows from adjectives and adverbs to the words they modify.
- Write *O.P.* over the object of a preposition.
- Enclose prepositional phrases within parentheses.
- Label each prepositional phrase with either *ADJ.* or *ADV.*
- Draw arrows from prepositional phrases to the words they modify.
- Use Noun Function Cards 1–5:
  Put an *S.* over each subject.
  Circle each direct object.
  Put *P.N.* above each predicate nominative.

1. Mr. LaChance is a politician (in Denver.)

2. Mother is very happy (with the new computer.)

3. The cute dog is a female poodle.

4. Dad found the (ball) (on the roof.)

5. Thomas Jefferson was the third president (of the United States.)

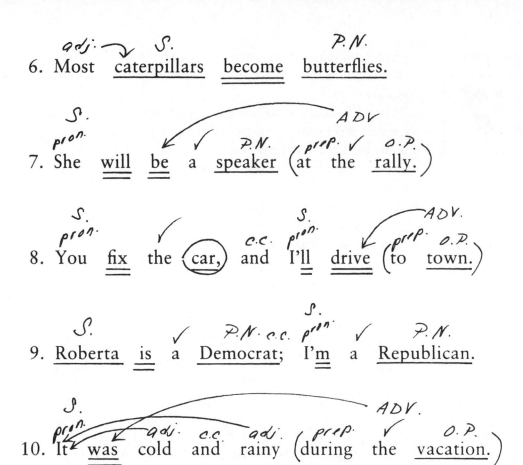

6. Most caterpillars become butterflies.
    adj.   *S.*   *P.N.*

7. She will be a speaker (at the rally.)
    S. *pron.*   ✓   *P.N.*   *prep.* ✓ *O.P.*   *ADV*

8. You fix the (car,) and I'll drive (to town.)
    S. *pron.*   ✓   *c.c.* *S. pron.*   ✓   *prep. O.P.*   *ADV.*

9. Roberta is a Democrat; I'm a Republican.
    S.   *is* ✓ *P.N. c.c.* *S. pron* ✓ *P.N.*

10. It was cold and rainy (during the vacation.)
    S. pron.   *adj. c.c. adj.*   *prep.* ✓ *O.P.*   *ADV.*

- Identify all parts of speech learned so far.
- If a pronoun has been omitted, write it in and enclose it within parentheses.
- Draw arrows from adjectives and adverbs to the words they modify.
- Write *O.P.* over the object of a preposition.
- Enclose prepositional phrases within parentheses.
- Label each prepositional phrase with either *ADJ.* or *ADV.*
- Draw arrows from prepositional phrases to the words they modify.
- Use Noun Function Cards 1–5:
    Put an *S.* over each subject.
    Circle each direct object.
    Put *P.N.* above each predicate nominative.

1. Diamonds and rubies are valuable gems.

2. Geese fly (from Canada) (to the southern United States)

(during the fall.)

3. She told me a good story.

4. Fire came (from the engine) (near the tip) (of the wing.)

5. I was shocked (by the news) (from Washington.)

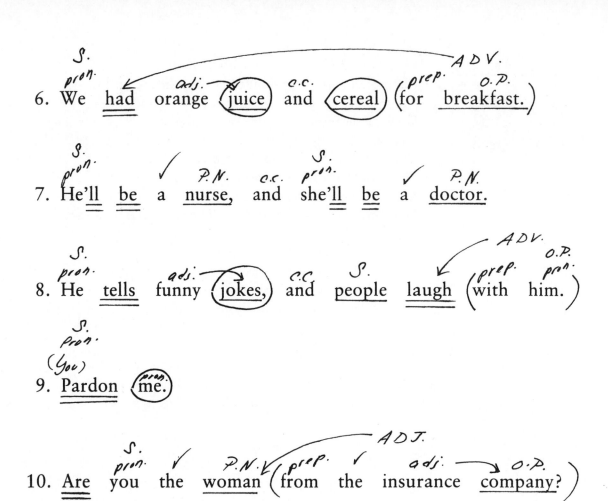

6. We had orange juice and cereal for breakfast.

7. He'll be a nurse, and she'll be a doctor.

8. He tells funny jokes, and people laugh with him.

9. Pardon me.

10. Are you the woman from the insurance company?

(to be taken after completing Worksheet 28)

- Identify all parts of speech learned so far.
- If a pronoun has been omitted, write it in and enclose it within parentheses.
- Draw arrows from adjectives and adverbs to the words they modify.
- Write *O.P.* over the object of a preposition.
- Enclose prepositional phrases within parentheses.
- Label each prepositional phrase with either *ADJ.* or *ADV.*
- Draw arrows from prepositional phrases to the words they modify.
- Use Noun Function Cards 1-5:
    - Put an *S.* over each subject.
    - Circle each direct object.
    - Put a box around each indirect object.
    - Put *P.N.* above each predicate nominative.

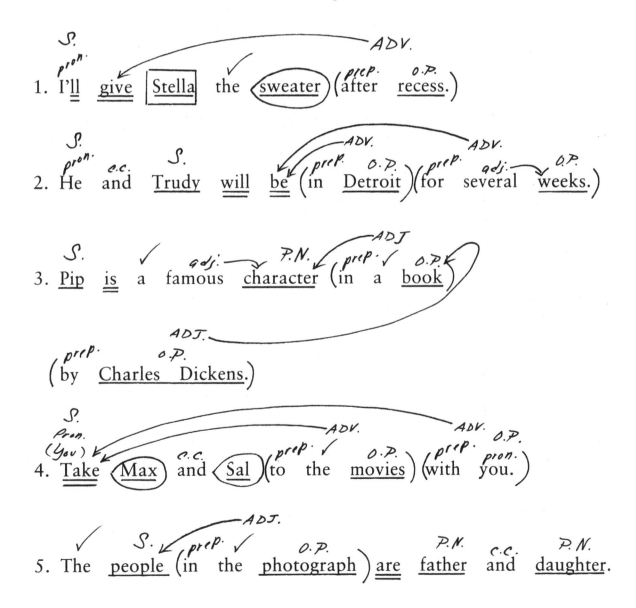

1. I'll give Stella the sweater (after recess.)

2. He and Trudy will be (in Detroit) (for several weeks.)

3. Pip is a famous character (in a book) (by Charles Dickens.)

4. Take Max and Sal (to the movies) (with you.)

5. The people (in the photograph) are father and daughter.

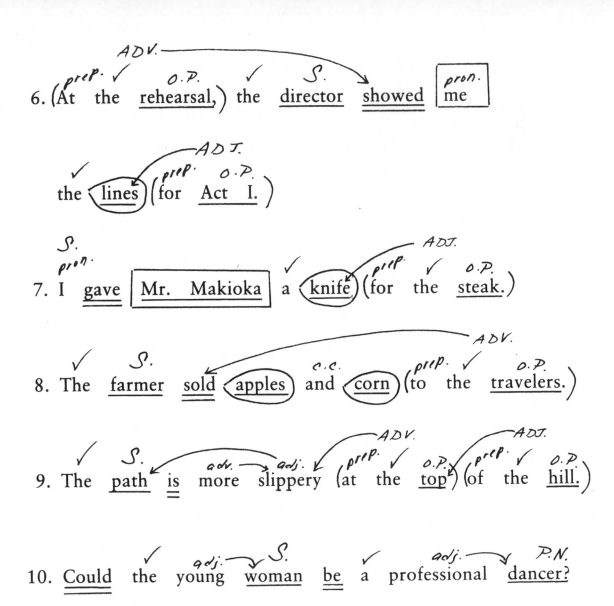

6. (At the rehearsal,) the director showed me
   the lines (for Act I.)

7. I gave Mr. Makioka a knife (for the steak.)

8. The farmer sold apples and corn (to the travelers.)

9. The path is more slippery (at the top) (of the hill.)

10. Could the young woman be a professional dancer?

Bonus

Alice's Adventures in Wonderland has become a
very famous book (for children and adults.)

- Identify all parts of speech learned so far.
- If a pronoun has been omitted, write it in and enclose it within parentheses.
- Draw arrows from adjectives and adverbs to the words they modify.
- Write *O.P.* over the object of a preposition.
- Enclose prepositional phrases within parentheses.
- Label each prepositional phrase with either *ADJ.* or *ADV.*
- Draw arrows from prepositional phrases to the words they modify.
- Use Noun Function Cards 1–7:
      Put an *S.* over each subject.
      Circle each direct object.
      Put *P.N.* above each predicate nominative.
      Write *N.D.A.* over nouns of direct address.

1. Will you come (with us) (to the airport,) Phillip?

2. A famous actor appears (in the film.)

3. Eva, have you finished the math yet?

4. Collect the trash (in the backyard,) Joe.
   (You)

5. Mack Burton mowed the soccer field.

6. Help Roger (with the luggage,) David.
   (You)

                    S.   c.c.   S.   adj.   adj.   P.N.
7. Cats   and   dogs   are   popular   house   pets.

              S.
      pron   adj.   adj.   adj.   P.N.
8. You   can't   become   a   good   tennis   player

              ADV.
      prep   O.P.
   (without   practice.)

      N.D.A.   S.   P.N.
                          pron.
9. Alberta,   are   you   a   Girl   Scout?

      S.   ADV.   ADV.
      pron.   prep.   O.P.   prep.   O.P.
10. We   went   (on   a   diet)(after   the   holidays.)

- Identify all parts of speech learned so far.
- Write in any pronouns that have been omitted and enclose them in parentheses.
- Draw arrows from adjectives and adverbs to the words they modify.
- Write *O.P.* over the object of a preposition.
- Enclose prepositional phrases within parentheses.
- Label each prepositional phrase with either *ADJ.* or *ADV.*
- Draw arrows from prepositional phrases to the words they modify.
- Use Noun Function Cards 1–8:
    Put an *S.* over each subject.
    Circle each direct object.
    Put *P.N.* above each predicate nominative.
    Write *N.D.A.* over nouns of direct address.
    Write *APP.* above each appositive.

1. The friendly mailman, Mr. Bettencourt, retired yesterday.

2. The only store (in town) will close soon.

3. The television show, *Sesame Street*, is popular (with many young children.)

4. Queen Victoria was a powerful ruler.

5. Katarina Kline, the chairperson, ended the meeting promptly.

6. The Tin Man is a character (in *The Wizard of Oz.*)
   √   S.   √   P.N. prep.   ADJ. O.P.

7. Buck became sheriff (of the county.)
   S.   P.N. prep. √ ADJ. O.P.

8. Be kind (to animals.)
   S. pron. (You) adv. ads. prep. O.P.
   ADV.

9. Louisa May Alcott is the author (of the book.)
   S.   √ P.N. prep. √ ADJ. O.P.

10. Turn the (corner,) but be careful, Pat.
    S. pron. (You) √ c.c. S. pron. (you) adj. N.D.A.

Posttest

Write your answers to the following questions on the lines at the right.

Sentence 1

The large bull charged angrily across the field.

1. Name the adjective.   *large*   1.
2. Name the adverb.   *angrily*   2.
3. Name the preposition.   *across*   3.
4. Name the subject.   *bull*   4.
5. Name the object of the preposition.   *field*   5.
6. What word does *angrily* modify?   *charged*   6.

Sentence 2

I sent Hal a long letter today.

7. Name the direct object.   *letter*   7.
8. Name the adverb.   *today*   8.
9. Name the verb.   *sent*   9.
10. Name the pronoun.   *I*   10.
11. Name the article.   *a*   11.
12. Name the indirect object.   *Hal*   12.
13. What word does *long* modify?   *letter*   13.

Sentence 3

Do not drink the soda before lunch, Nancy.

14. How many nouns are there in Sentence 3?	*three*	14.
15. Name the direct object.	*soda*	15.
16. Name the noun of direct address.	*Nancy*	16.
17. Name the subject.	*(you)*	17.
18. Name the verb and helping verb.	*do drink*	18.
19. Name the adverb.	*not*	19.

Sentence 4

We are afraid of the snake, and I wish it would disappear.

20. Name the coordinating conjunction.	*and*	20.
21. Name the helping verb.	*would*	21.
22. Name the "being" or "linking" verb.	*are*	22.
23. How many subjects are there in Sentence 4?	*three*	23.
24. Name the adjective.	*afraid*	24.

Sentence 5

Wow, the story is really scary!

25. Name the verb.	*is*	25.
26. Name the adverb.	*really*	26.
27. Name the interjection.	*Wow*	27.
28. Name the article.	*the*	28.

Sentence 6

She and Lorenzo were the best actors in the school play.

29. How many adjectives are there in Sentence 6?	*two*	29.
30. Name the object of the preposition.	*play*	30.
31. Name the subject(s).	*She, Lorenzo*	31.
32. Name the predicate nominative.	*actors*	32.
33. What part of speech is *school*?	*adjective*	33.